WHAT PEOPL

MW00804404

"In her groundbreaking new book, Dr. Hollingsworth addresses a critical leadership challenge of our time: the pressing need for enhanced empathy and emotional intelligence in leadership. She equips organizational leaders with the insights and motivation necessary to foster stronger, more meaningful connections between leaders and staff. This book is an indispensable resource for improving collaboration, building trust, enhancing accountability, and ensuring that everyone feels valued, respected, and included. It's a must-read for any leader committed to this transformative journey."
— Dr. Ramon A. Pastrano, GCL, MSM, CO-USNR

"In *The Compassion Advantage*, Andrea Hollingsworth, Ph.D., delves into the transformative power of compassionate leadership. This book is an essential guide for leaders aiming to build more humanizing and resilient workplaces. Hollingsworth combines evidence-based insights with practical strategies to show how compassion enhances employee well-being, engagement, growth and productivity. Featuring real stories and actionable advice, this book demonstrates that compassion is a skill that can be learned and developed. Leaders will find inspiration to cultivate empathy, mindfulness, and compassionate action, fostering a culture where both people and businesses thrive.

As a progressive and integral leader featured in this work, I can attest to the profound impact compassionate leadership can have on organizational success and human flourishing."
— Clinton Goodwin, Chief Operating Officer
Fujitsu General Australia

"Walking the leadership journey described in these pages will instill strength, stability, resilience, trust, and belonging in yourself. This book is essential for leaders who want to balance caring connection with decisive accountability."
— Dan Riley, Co-founder, Radicl

"Thoughtful and relevant! We need *The Compassion Advantage* more than ever in our world today. Thank you, Dr. Andrea Hollingsworth for providing a roadmap for leaders committed to instilling cultures of connection and trust while accelerating business performance. The stories, science, and strategies in this book can transform how you think about leadership in an increasingly volatile and wounding world."
— Dr. David Horsager, CEO, TrustEdge Leadership Institute

"Reading Andrea's book will leave you forever changed for the better. With every page you will feel like you are spending time with a smart, witty best friend, who is your cheerleader in becoming a more compassionate leader and human. Andrea does a brilliant job of balancing stories and anecdotes, while weaving in scholarly research to make sure her guidance is not based on gut and good intentions, but also very strong facts. If you are looking for both motivation and practical tips for becoming more compassionate, Andrea's book is a must-read."
— Dr. Sanja Licina, President, QuestionPro Workforce

THE
COMPASSION
ADVANTAGE

How Top Leaders Build More Humanizing Workplaces

Andrea Hollingsworth, Ph.D.

Copyright © 2024 Andrea Hollingsworth
All rights reserved.

No part of this book may be reproduced or utilized in any form or by any means, electronic or mechanical, including photocopying, recording, or by any information storage retrieval system without permission in writing from the publisher, with the exception of a reviewer who may quote brief passages in a review.

Hollingsworth Consulting
6417 Penn Ave. Ste. 7
Minneapolis, MN 55423-1196
www.hollingsworthconsulting.com

Cover design: Murshidi Mahmud
Interior design: Julie Murkette

ISBN: 979-8-9908633-0-9 paperback
ISBN: 979-8-9908633-1-6 hardcover
ISBN: 979-8-9908633-2-3 eBook

Publisher's Cataloging-in-Publication Data

Names: Hollingsworth, Andrea, author.
Title: The compassion advantage : how top leaders build more humanizing workplaces / Andrea Hollingsworth, PhD.
Description: Includes bibliographical records. | Minneapolis, MN: Hollingsworth Consulting, 2024.
Identifiers: LCCN: xxxxxxxxx | ISBN: 979-8-9908633-1-6 (hardcover) | 979-8-9908633-0-9 (paperback) | 979-8-9908633-2-3 (ebook)
Subjects: LCSH Leadership. | Leadership--Psychological aspects. | Leadership--Social aspects. | Compassion. | Management. | Corporate culture. | Success in business. | Business communication. | BISAC BUSINESS & ECONOMICS / Leadership | BUSINESS & ECONOMICS / Workplace Culture
Classification: LCC HD57.7 .H65 2024 | DDC 658.4--dc23

Note: *The information presented in this book is in no way intended as medical advice or as a substitute for medical, psychological, or other counseling. If you have medical or psychological concerns, consult your doctor or a qualified health care professional.*

ACKNOWLEDGMENTS

I've written and published many things over the years. Of all the pieces I've created, this book has, by far, brought me the most joy. It's been so much fun translating the knowledge and wisdom gleaned from my former academic career into a book that speaks to everyone, not just those in proverbial ivory towers.

I have many people to thank for their help and encouragement.

My dear friend, Fern Braam, served as my accountability buddy during the writing process. On the first day of every month, at least one new chapter was "due" in Fern's inbox. She usually read the chapter(s) that very day, providing excellent feedback and letting me know she was eager for more. There's no way I would've produced the book with such swiftness and ease were it not for Fern.

Over the course of her nine-month internship with Hollingsworth Consulting, McCall Dubbelman dedicated many hours of research, writing, and editing. Her efforts enhanced this book in untold ways. As well, Julie Murkette provided swift and skilled editing assistance, and helped greatly with the logistics of the self-publishing process.

As I wrote, I had the privilege of interviewing various leaders and hearing their inspiring stories of compassionate leadership. Many of those stories are included in the pages that follow. For their time, insights, and stories, I thank Jessica Kasper, Eric Owski, Nicole Pullen, Clinton Goodwin, Rushmie Nofsinger, Sanja Licina, David Miller, Kelli Moretter-Bue, and Ramona Sequeira, among others. Although I did not interview her personally, Pamela Maynard's recorded conversation with Jacqueline Carter and Julie Devoll on March 10, 2023 was an incredible resource and gift.

This book is laced with the wisdom and inspiration I've received from the many clients I've been honored to serve in consulting, speaking, and coaching roles. I'm particularly grateful to Robin Downing and the leaders at City and County Credit Union;

Carrie Heimer and the leaders at Red Wing Shoe Company; Kyle Severson and the leaders at Chicagoland ELCA; Amy Klein and the leaders at the North Dakota Court System; and Ramona Sequeira and the leaders at Takeda.

I have the best mentors and advisors an aspiring speaker/consultant/author could ask for! To Ramón Pastrano, David Horsager, Mark Silver and, more recently, Simone Ahuja and Dan Riley: thank you for your sage advice and steadfast support along the way.

And to the many wonderful family members and friends who cheered me on as I wrote: your presence in my life buoys and energizes me so much! Special thanks to Ryan Hollingsworth, Heidi Bauer, Brent Johnson, Michelle Johnson, Jake Botkins, Kelli Morretter-Bue, and Heather Boschke.

Finally, my son Bennett Hollingsworth was a tremendous source of inspiration and hope as I wrote. Bennett: at the tender age of seven, I already see you becoming exactly the kind of compassionate leader the world needs—both now and in the future. This book is dedicated to you.

To my son, Bennett,
whose compassion is his superpower.

The Compassion Advantage

TABLE OF CONTENTS

Introduction
The Great Dispiriting

About three years after the onset of the Covid-19 global pandemic, I was asked to speak to a group of top-level business executives on "Quiet Quitting." These leaders were deeply concerned about the growing trend, which had exploded on TikTok in 2022 and pointed to profound worker disengagement. Like other executives,[1] those in this group wondered: "What if there's a major recession and I can't rely on my employees?" "How can I spot quiet quitters in my organization?" "Will I be forced to keep paying people who are chronically underperforming?"

I was committed to helping these leaders pinpoint strategies for re-engaging their employees. I needed to show them I understood their worries. So, for my talk's headline, I chose "Would you Please Just Do Your Job?"

The title struck a chord with them. Why? Because the troubled C-suite leaders in this group felt frustrated. Their inward thoughts toward their quiet quitters sounded something like this: "Look. I hired you to lean into your potential, to go above and beyond, to work with that burn in your belly. When you do the bare bones minimum, when you settle for perpetual settling, you're not doing the job I hired you to do. *Please*. Can you find it in you to *care*, here? Just a little?"

Yet, what if I'd been speaking to a different audience? Say—a room full of burnt out and "over it" Millennial and Gen-Z employees? In that case, I would have titled the talk "Would you

Please Just Respect My Boundaries?" Why? Because today's quiet quitters are frustrated, too. If they had their druthers, they'd tell their bosses something like this: "Look. I'm done meeting your demands of constant peak performance. Can you just revisit the basics of my job description and get off my back? Isn't 'good enough' good enough? I'm doing the best I can. *Please.* Can you find it in you to *care*, here? Just a little?"

Two takes, one problem.

And there is a problem—that's undeniable. According to Gallup, fully half of U.S. workers fall into the category of quiet quitters—folks who stay in their position, but only take care of job essentials.[2] Recent employment and productivity numbers bear that out. In 2022, while employment in nonfarm business grew at an impressive annual rate of 4.3 percent, labor productivity plummeted, falling at a historic 6 percent annual rate.[3] The labor productivity drop-off continued into 2023,[4] with more people being hired but less work being done. Researchers at George Washington University emphasize that "quiet quitting" is neither hype nor a passing phase. It's a quantifiable phenomenon, and it's likely to continue—especially among younger, educated workers.[5]

Something real is happening in the collective psyche of today's workforce. It's like a cloud of apathy, resentment, and exhaustion has descended on employees everywhere. What's going on? Wouldn't it be amazing if we could find a common denominator to this Great Dispiriting? Maybe then we could get some traction on a solution.

Pain is the Problem, Compassion is the Solution

Over the last few years, I've been listening intently to top business leaders and consultants, Human Resource professionals, and managers across business sectors. I've also been paying close attention to my therapy clients, most of whom are members of the workforce, and I've been researching—*a lot.*

All this strategic listening and careful inquiry has convinced me of one thing, and it's this: *Disengaged employees are in pain.*

Everywhere we are witnessing the effects of a vast societal crisis of emotional distress and mental exhaustion. For some, it's acute and disabling. For others, it's more like the background ache of osteoarthritis. Even if we're not depressed per se, many of us are, as Adam Grant has famously pointed out, "languishing."[6] It's hard to rise above *meh* in any domain, including work. Why? Because our nervous systems feel beaten down by the unending barrage of VUCA[7] from so many spheres—economic, political, socio-cultural, and more.

As I'll later explain, this beaten-down feeling is evidence of our collective post-2020 trauma, and it's impacting everything. It affects our neighborhoods, homes, places of worship, families, and of course, our workplaces. Vast numbers of people are softly (or sharply) pulling back from life because the last handful of years have left them wounded, wearied, angry, and on edge. *This* is what today's chronic and widespread employee disengagement and burnout is all about.

The solution? *Compassion.*

Compassionate human connections revive and empower. They heal trauma at both individual and collective levels. When leaders cultivate authentic compassion in themselves and their organizational culture, it allows people to show up with renewed interest, energy, and dedication. As I'll later explain, this renewed vitality isn't a rational decision people make. Rather, it's a biologically based response of the human nervous system. When a hurt and overwhelmed human brain detects that it's been placed in an environment of safety and care, it can crawl out of survival mode and get back in the game.

It's sometimes assumed that compassionate leaders are spineless and ineffective, but nothing could be further from the truth. As we'll see, research shows that compassionate leaders are highly skilled, action-oriented powerhouses who courageously create conditions of connection and trust. Compassion bolsters retention, drives innovation, supercharges engagement, and attracts top talent. If we want to re-ignite, re-commit, and re-enliven a languishing

American workforce, we need more compassionate organizational leaders, and we need more compassionate work cultures overall.

That is the basic argument of this book.

In the coming chapters, I will lead you on a journey of understanding:

1. *Why* compassionate leadership is needed in today's organizations;

2. *What* the impact of compassionate leadership looks like, both fiscally and psychologically; and

3. *How* to instill a culture of compassion in your organization.

I will show you why and how prioritizing compassion will help solve one of the most serious problems facing businesses today: working people are suffering. They're suffering in numbers and to degrees we've not before seen, and it's affecting all facets of organizational life, including morale, engagement, performance, productivity, and revenue. In such a context, effective, transformative leadership means courageously taking on a whole new skill set.

Yes, I said "skill set." Compassion isn't a personality trait you either have or don't have. It's a core competency that people can learn.

With inspiration, know-how, tools, and practice, compassion can be infused into an organization's culture, goals, and strategy. When that happens, it propels measurable, powerful results.

The Compassion Advantage

Compassion is sometimes deemed a "soft skill" in management practice. In truth, there's nothing "soft" about it. In their research on compassionate leadership practices, Hougaard and Carter[8] have shown that heartfelt care without the willingness to say and do hard things isn't compassionate. Rather, it's gutless and inept. Conversely, readiness to say and do hard things without heartfelt care isn't compassionate. Rather, it's alienating and ineffectual.

When you're a leader with both heart and backbone, you're a compassionate leader. As such, you sit more in the category of brave badass than fragile flower. Why? Because while your power and position probably give you permission to not care, you intentionally choose to look pain in the face and then do something about it. There is incredible strength, respectability, and influence in that approach. It makes people feel seen, safe, and supported. When they feel those things, they can exit survival mode and start firing on all cylinders again.

Leaders who can make people feel safe enough to heal and reengage have always had an advantage. This is especially true in times of stress, turmoil, or change. In the words of Dr. Jane Dutton, a pioneering researcher in the field of compassionate leadership:

> A leader's ability to enable a compassionate response throughout a company directly affects the organization's ability to maintain high performance in difficult times. [...] When people know they can bring their pain to the office, they no longer have to expend energy trying to ignore or suppress it, and they can more easily and effectively get back to work.[9]

Dutton wrote that almost a quarter century ago, in the wake of the events of 9/11, and recent research proves her words perennially true. As we'll later see, compassionate leadership in organizations helps create environments of psychological safety in which people feel connected, supported, and genuinely cared for. Compassion heightens employee satisfaction and commitment, strengthens relationships, reduces turnover, boosts employee morale and engagement, and increases levels of creativity and innovation. All this affects the bottom line by slashing costs associated with employee turnover, burnout, and disengagement.

When fearless and inspirational leaders commit to building a culture of care in their organization, significant and measurable value accrues. That's *The Compassion Advantage*.

About This Book

If you're looking to invest in the sort of mindset and culture change that breathes vibrancy, trust, and commitment back into your organization in times of challenge and change, this book is for you. Consider it your roadmap for creating an organizational environment where the people of today—people who've suffered and survived so much recently—can begin to thrive again at work, even or especially in times of ongoing difficulty and flux.

This book is divided into five main sections. Part I focuses on the *why*. Here I present an evidence-based, trauma-informed, neurobiologically-oriented, and business-minded argument for the vital necessity of compassionate leadership in our current context.

The next four sections detail the *how*. There are four elements of compassionate leadership, and in Parts II–V, I treat each one in turn.

Everything begins with *self-compassion* (Part II). Many leaders have a muscled-up inner bully that no one else sees or hears. Learning to quiet the voice of your inner critic through self-attunement, self-connection, and self-advocacy gives you the wisdom and wherewithal you need to show up strong for others.

Mindful *awareness* (Part III) is the second element of compassionate leadership. This section teaches you practical ways to still your mind, soothe your body, and focus your attention on the here and now. From this powerfully grounded state, your awareness and understanding of others both expands and deepens. People begin to experience you as truly, fully *present*—a quality that's less and less common in our distraction-saturated world.

The third element of compassionate leadership is *empathy* (Part IV). In this section, you'll first learn about the neuroscience of emotionally resonant human connection. You'll also gain inspiration, skills, and strategies for living and leading in a way that's powerfully connected with others, yet also with appropriate boundaries.

Compassionate leadership hinges on the fourth element, *action* (Part V). This last section provides invaluable tools for *doing something* to help mitigate unnecessary suffering amongst those you lead. You'll walk away with strategies for fostering a culture of compassionate accountability in which hard things are communicated in connected, genuine, and human ways. You will also learn how to lead with compassion in situations of conflict and collective trauma.

This book can be utilized in many ways. Whether you read it straight through or focus on particular sections and chapters, you'll gain transformative insights and strategies that will empower you to show up strong for yourself and those in your charge. The book is especially valuable when read in a group setting or team learning and development context. Each chapter presents stories, studies, insights, and actionable suggestions that spur conversation and growth. Discussion questions at the close of each chapter can be utilized to guide dialogue and reflection.

Whichever way(s) you choose to engage the book you hold in your hands, may it inspire and equip you to instill cultures of caring, trustful connection wherever you lead—to the great benefit of you, those around you, and our shared world.

Part I
The Case for Compassion

Chapter 1
What's the Issue, Dear?

At the time of this writing, I'm the mom of a kindergartener, which means there's a whole lot of Disney going on in my home. At this point I think I know both *Frozen*'s by heart, heaven help me. In the first one, there's a scene where a matchmaker troll is trying to get a princess engaged to a local outdoorsman, but the princess really isn't feeling it. "*What's the issue,* dear?" the troll eggs on the princess. "Why are you holding back from such a *man?*"

A lot of employers are sort of like this troll. They're desperate to know, "What's the issue? What's keeping you from getting engaged? Why are you holding back? Look—look at this sexy benefits package! *Come and get it.* Here—here's some monetary incentive! *You know you want it.* Come *on*, where's your spark?" Actually, a lot of employees are asking the same basic questions of themselves. "What the hell is going on with me? I used to care about excelling at work. Now I can't even bring myself to *want* to care. Where *is* my spark?"

Here's what's true. As individuals and as a society, we're still trying to emerge from one of the most traumatizing moments in modern history. First, there was the Covid-19 pandemic. Think back to how you first felt—locked in your house, homeschooling your kids, bleaching your milk cartons, stockpiling toilet paper, and trying your best to figure out this new video conferencing technology. It was completely bonkers. We're not in that moment anymore, but the stressful societal events do keep coming. We can't seem to catch our breath. Political unrest, the economy, racism, the mental health crisis, climate catastrophes, school shootings, global conflict: it simply doesn't stop.

What's the issue, dear? The issue is that while our rational minds are telling us we should get re-engaged with work and just move on, the more primitive parts of our nervous systems would like a word. *Wait—wait a minute. What just happened? You're saying it's safe now? It sure doesn't feel safe!*

The point is that we are, personally and collectively, still very much traumatized. Trauma can happen anytime we are forced into dangerous and/or difficult situations wherein we feel helpless, responsible, and alone. Our minds and bodies adjust accordingly, just as evolutionary history has taught them to do. Stress chemicals like cortisol and adrenaline pump through our veins, preparing us to fight, flee, freeze, or fawn. We become either more vigilant and anxious, or more apathetic and checked out. Because our brains have shifted into survival mode, our executive functioning takes a big hit. We're less able to focus, plan, organize, create. It's harder to calm down, exercise restraint, be courteous, and stay motivated. It seems most of our energy goes toward just getting by and bracing ourselves for the next thing. Beyond that, there's not much left.

In addition to collective trauma, I believe we're grieving, as well. We grieve the loss of a time when we saw fewer screens and more flesh-and-blood faces; when things seemed a touch more stable, civil, and respectful. We grieve the growing cracks and dysfunctions in social structures we assumed (or at least hoped) we could count on. In important ways, the world feels less and less familiar. So, the unmistakable symptoms of grief and loss start to weigh us down. Our immune systems weaken. Our bodies inflame. We have trouble thinking, sleeping, conversing. We're irritable and forgetful. We feel like we can't cope.

When underlying trauma and grief become the baseline state in which many people have come to call home, it's going to show up in the workplace.

And it has.

Fresh Out of Bandwidth

Matt is an ER nurse who's stopped caring that he no longer makes eye contact with his patients. Yeah, he'll change your fluid bag when he can get to it, but no niceties. Why? Well, it sucks to connect with someone you know you're going to piss off later. (You know, after they push their red call button, but you can't help them for another hour because you're flooded with other extremely urgent and maximally stressful tasks.) Matt knows he comes off as an asshole nurse. He just doesn't have the bandwidth to care.

Matt is not alone. He's one of millions of workers globally whose stress levels are deeply affecting their work engagement and performance. In 2020, ComPsych surveyed employees across America, and found that an astounding 62% had high levels of stress, with extreme fatigue and feeling out of control. Of those surveyed, 59% said their top work priority was merely accomplishing basic responsibilities, rather than being present or improving performance.[10] Another report from Qualtrics[11] found that 67% of global workers reported increases in stress, with 54% saying they felt emotionally exhausted. While it's true that those findings reflect the initial shock of the pandemic, the worker stress crisis has not abated. In 2023, the Gallup World Poll revealed that stress among working people across the globe is at a record high since Gallup began collecting data from adult employees in 2005.[12]

Melissa is a manager at a local hardware store who's stopped caring that more and more of her employees are quitting, no-showing, or coming to work drunk or stoned. Why? Truth is, she herself has become dependent on a daily concoction of Sudafed, alcohol, and pain pills to cope with life. As a single mom to twin kindergarteners with special needs in an underfunded school district, Melissa's stress levels are through the roof. She knows she needs better ways of managing her stress (and accompanying anxiety symptoms) than with chemicals, but she doesn't have the bandwidth to care.

Melissa is not alone. Gallup[13] finds that among U.S. and Canadian workers, women are under the most pressure, with 57% reporting daily feelings of stress. This is linked to gendered caregiving expectations and childcare challenges, and women's overrepresentation in low wage service jobs. Anxiety symptoms are soaring among workers, too—both men and women alike. According to the Anxiety and Depression Association of America, 40% of U.S. employees say excessive anxiety is a part of their daily life, with almost a third reporting an anxiety or panic attack.[14] Many people self-medicate to relieve symptoms of high stress and accompanying anxiety. Versta Research has found that 49% of U.S. workers report struggling with some kind of substance addiction,[15] with nearly one out of four people admitting to using drugs or alcohol on the job.[16]

Felicity is a work-from-home senior accountant who's stopped caring that her usual 30-minute lunch breaks have turned into a 90-minute lunch + nap + social media breaks. Why? Lately Felicity has been so drained and depressed that it's all she can do to roll out of bed, fire up her computer, and hope her Red Bull keeps her going until she can shut her eyes again at noon. Felicity knows she's a star underperformer, but she doesn't have the bandwidth to care.

Felicity is not alone. Nearly four in ten American workers report feeling a lack of motivation along with symptoms of depression,[17] including fatigue, difficulty concentrating, loss of interest in things, feelings of hopelessness, and difficulty sleeping. Among Americans who recently left their job, 89% report feeling burnt out—that is, irritable, lacking in energy, unfocused, and unmotivated.

There's a pall of sadness, lassitude, and listlessness that's crept over the hearts and bodies of many working people. You notice when they call in sick (yet again). You notice it when they keep their camera off during the remote team huddle. You notice it when they protest the slightest procedural change, and sometimes, when you get a chance to see their face and look into their eyes, you see it quite clearly.

What does leadership look like in a low-bandwidth world? How do you guide, encourage, coordinate, and rouse when those you lead (and perhaps you, yourself) are running on fumes?

In an environment where people are wounded and in survival mode, leadership requires a whole new approach. Our toolkits are outdated; the things we used to use to motivate and inspire no longer work. You can't optimize strengths when folks are awash in apathy. You can't inspire innovation when people are barely getting by. You can't beef it up, crush it clean, make it pop, dive in deep, and raise the bar when many or most of your people would be thrilled simply to get back to good.

Wise leaders meet people where they're at and create conditions that will help them get to a better place. When workers are as wounded as they are currently, it's time to start mapping out what a courageously compassionate leadership presence and practice might look like. What does it take to be the sort of leader that helps people get back to good, and then, to great? That question is exactly the one I aim to explore in the pages that follow.

But wait! Maybe you've noticed I haven't yet explained what compassion even *is!* I used to be a full-time academic, which means definitions matter to me—probably a bit too much. So before going any further, let's pause to get some conceptual clarity on compassion.

Discussion Questions

1. Can you think of an example from your own experience (or perhaps someone in your workplace) regarding facing significant overwhelm, stress, low bandwidth, or other, similar challenges?

2. Can you describe instances where you have effectively managed and rejuvenated your mental and emotional energy?

3. Can you think of a leader, either from your personal or professional life, who you consider to be exemplary? What specific qualities or actions make them stand out as a great leader? How have they influenced and inspired you?

CHAPTER 2
FOUR THINGS COMPASSION IS NOT

"How often should I cry-hug my team members?"

It was break time at a training I was doing on compassionate leadership for a group of banking professionals. We'd all just finished a lively conversation about the psychological, cultural, and fiscal benefits of a compassionate work environment. Hakeem, a regional branch manager, had pulled me aside. He was fully on board the compassionate leadership boat, but he just needed to know one thing. Precisely *how* touchy-feely should he get with his people, and *how often* should that happen? What kind of cry-hug schedule should he set, here?

Hakeem's question highlights the complexity and confusion that surrounds the notion of compassion. It is, after all, an ancient concept with many meanings. In Buddhist wisdom traditions, compassion is often linked to the intentional awareness of suffering, and the active wish for its alleviation. In western philosophy and religion, the emphasis is often on Christ's suffering and the implications for humanity. Compassion also has a robust presence in modern psychology and related disciplines, where its scientific meaning usually includes both an affective and a behavioral component.

Yet, how should we think about compassion in a business and management context?

I told Hakeem that while tearful embraces may happen occasionally in a professional setting (for example, in cases of traumatic events or losses), emotive hug fests are peripheral to what I'm getting at. *When I talk about compassionate leadership, I mean a commitment to building workplace cultures that prioritize caring connection and practical support.*

Now, is the practice of emotional attunement part of that intentional commitment? Absolutely. However, I know very few managers who would deem it appropriate and helpful to cry-hug a team member. That's actually *not* a practice I would readily recommend, and I'll explain why in Chapter 10. The picture is much larger—much more strategic and multifaceted—than shared waterworks.

There are, clearly, many misconceptions of what compassion means. To understand the essence of compassion in our context, it will help to acknowledge what it *isn't*.

Compassion Isn't Empathy

People use these terms interchangeably, which is fine in the context of everyday conversation, but strictly speaking, empathy and compassion aren't the same. Empathy simply means feeling with someone, whatever they're experiencing—whether good or bad. Compassion, though, is a narrower term. Stemming from the Latin words *cum* + *pati* (meaning "to suffer with"), compassion means feeling with someone who's in pain. I can have empathy for you if you're eating an apple, but I can only have compassion for you if you're in distress while you eat it. (Perhaps you have a toothache, or it's mealy, or you found a dead worm inside.)

Another crucial difference between empathy and compassion is that the latter includes an active component. Compassion involves *doing something* to relieve suffering. Advocacy is intrinsic to its meaning. Compassion doesn't stop at emotional resonance; it is intelligent and strategic about helping ease pain and bring about betterment.

Compassion Isn't a Fixed Personality Trait

It's not something you either have or don't have. Rather, compassion is a core leadership competency that can be developed and honed.

When I was growing up, my dad wasn't always compassionate. In fact, throughout his youth and middle age, he was quite rough and tough—especially verbally. He didn't have time for your bellyaching. If you were sick, it was "all in your head." As he aged, however, his emotional literacy improved. He started saying things like, "You know, I've learned it's much better to listen than to speak." He started calling me regularly to ask about what I was studying in my Ph.D. program. He began finding creative ways to encourage me when I felt overwhelmed. Dad actively—consciously—*worked* to become more compassionate, and it changed him (and those around him) for the better.

My dad's experience reflects the amazing discoveries cognitive neuroscientists have made in the last several decades. Neuroimaging studies strongly suggest that regularly engaging in certain compassion practices can alter both the structure and function of the brain. Practicing mindful compassion correlates with increased gray matter and stronger synaptic connections in brain areas responsible for attention, empathy, emotion regulation, attachment, decision making, prioritization, and altruistic action. Compassion may come more naturally to some people than others. However, it is, unquestionably, a neurobiologically mediated skill that can be developed. Anyone who's willing, committed, and properly guided can become more compassionate.

Compassion Isn't Pity

This is for two reasons. First, pity looks at pain from a distance, whereas compassion risks getting in there. There's a wise and boundary-conscious *involvedness* that comes with compassion. It's the difference between saying, "Oh, you poor thing, how dreadful! I'll be over here feeling sorry for you" (pity), versus, "Hey, we're all human, we all have to ride the struggle bus sometimes. I feel you, and I'm going to do what I can to support you in this" (compassion). Secondly, pity reduces the sufferer to just their pain, whereas compassion sees the whole person. When people are struggling at work, there are always a great many variables at play. A compassionate manager will take the time to understand and strategize around those variables, but also to view the person in light of their strengths, potentials, and capacities for resilience. Compassion makes someone feel humanized, validated, and empowered. Pity makes someone feel like hurt is all they've got.

Compassion Isn't Weak

According to clinical psychologist Paul Gilbert, the essence of compassion isn't kindness, it's *courage*.[18] He's right. It takes a good deal more badassery to look pain in the face, express support, and implement a plan for wellness than it does to ignore the pain and hope it will go away on its own.

Let's face it: leaders have to say and do difficult, unpopular things. Whether it's having a corrective conversation, communicating news of a layoff, announcing a project re-do, or telling someone they were denied their requested PTO days: there are times when leaders must themselves *cause* individual suffering for the sake of the greater good. As Hougard and Carter have argued so beautifully, compassionate leaders "do hard things in a human way."[19] *When* they deliver tough news, they lean in instead of shutting down. *When* they make unpopular decisions, they choose connected dialogue over mechanistic indifference.

There's nothing "weak" or "soft" about leaders who insist on making their organization a place where people can be fully human, no matter the difficulty of the situation. As Kevin Sneader, global managing partner of McKinsey & Company puts it, compassionate leadership means "becoming colder and kinder at the same time."[20] It's about having the courage to balance an exacting mind with an open heart, and the wisdom to work toward integrating the two.

Discussion Questions

1. After learning about the "Four Things Compassion Is Not," were there any misconceptions that stood out to you? How did the information in this chapter shift your perceptions about what compassionate leadership is (and isn't)?

2. How do you interpret the notion that compassion requires courage rather than being synonymous with weakness? Can you think of examples where leaders have demonstrated this courage by making difficult decisions or delivering tough news in a compassionate and human-centered manner?

Chapter 3
This is Your Brain on Compassion

Let's say you catch a vision for producing an elegant, useful phone app that millions will use daily to enhance their life. So, you decide to found a tech company.

As you begin hiring your first employees and setting up personnel management practices, what baseline principle would you choose to define your new company culture? What would be your primary *premise* for attracting, motivating, and keeping the best people in your exciting and promising new organization? Would it be:

- *Money:* People who work here will be high-potential individuals who can count on being exceptionally compensated.

- *Professionalism:* People who work here will be outstandingly skilled specialists who can count on being exceptionally challenged.

- *Love:* People who work here will be highly fitted with others on the team, and can count on being exceptionally cared for.

In the late 1990's and early 2000's, sociologists James N. Baron and Michael T. Hannan wondered which founding premise would correlate with the most success. They tracked 200 tech startups in Silicon Valley, examining how the founders' underlying ideas about culture impacted business outcomes.

Only 13.9% of the startups prioritized love as a founding premise for company culture and people management. As it turns out, this minority group significantly outperformed the other groups. When founders focused on building strong emotional bonds and shared values amongst personnel, they saw striking results in revenue and longevity as compared to the other groups. They also got initial offerings three times more often when they went public.[21]

Leaders of highly impactful and long-lasting organizations know that love is the secret sauce of success. When work culture is built upon bonds of belonging and care—in a word, compassion—it sets the stage for magic.

Why?

Well, a lot has to do with the architecture of the squishy stuff inside our skulls. The human brain has evolved to fear rejection, punishment, abandonment, shaming, and other negative behaviors coming from our social group. After all, in our ancestral past, these types of experiences could kill us. Being ousted from the group was a death sentence if you were part of a Paleolithic hunter-gatherer tribe.

Fear-based social vigilance is cognitively expensive, though. It's stressful and mentally exhausting to be creative and high performing in an uncertain, unwelcoming, and threatening social setting. This is the whole reason behind the wild success of Chef Gordon Ramsay's show, *Hell's Kitchen*.

No, our brains thrive in settings where there's emotional safety, connection, closeness, and support. A culture of care and compassion means the social threats we most fear (like rejection, punishment, abandonment, and shame) are off the table. This means we're not spending our precious neurocognitive resources on social hedging. Plus, we know that if we're struggling, someone's got our back. Neurocognitively, this means three things:

1. Our brainstem-based threat detection systems are deactivated. This feels like the relief of letting down your guard.

2. Our limbic-based affiliative systems are engaged. This feels like the joyful comfort of having a "second family" at work.

3. Our prefrontal-based executive systems are fired up. This feels like the easy flow of focus, creativity, productivity, and problem-solving.

Organizations that prioritize love and compassion do better because human brains need safe, trustful, close emotional bonds to be at their best. This is especially true when people are struggling to recover from trauma, burnout, and overwhelm.

When caring, connected bonds are the backdrop of our working world, we stop worrying. We feel good. We show up. We work hard. We lean in. We take risks. We laugh and smile. In a word, we flourish—and so do the companies for which we work.

"But wait," you might be thinking, "it seems like many folks are simply not *wired* to be compassionate." Ever met a manager or executive leader who's too anxious, too judgmental, too oblivious, or too self-absorbed to experience and extend caring emotional bonds at work? Yeah. There are too many of those folks out there.

So, the next thing we need to know is this. Is compassion something you either have or don't have? Or can it be taught and developed over time – kind of like a good golf swing? If so, is there science to prove it?

Brain Sculpting

In 2013-2014, I had the honor of being a research fellow at a Princeton-based interdisciplinary think tank. It was a life-changing year for me, as I was part of a diverse research team investigating dimensions of moral identity. When I arrived that fall, the talk of the team was a ground-breaking new study,[22] hot off the press, conducted by a young researcher named Helen Weng at the University of Wisconsin-Madison.

In the study, one group of young adults underwent a brief training in compassion meditation—an ancient Buddhist technique where you envision bestowing lovingkindness upon yourself, a friend, a stranger, and finally, an enemy. Phrases are repeated during the meditation, such as, "May you be free from suffering. May you have joy and ease." Another group was trained in "cognitive reappraisal," where you simply learn to reframe negative thoughts and feelings.

After the trainings, participants were tested in two ways. First, they played a game in which they were given the opportunity to spend their own money to help someone in need. Second, they were put in an *f*MRI brain scanner while they observed photographs depicting human suffering, such as a crying child or a burn victim.

The group that had undergone compassion training stood out from the other group. Significantly. First, they were much more willing to donate their money to people in need. In other words, the compassion training appeared to make them more inclined to actively help others. Second, their brains responded differently to the photographs. Areas responsible for empathy, emotion regulation, and positive emotion showed significantly increased activity, as compared to the control group.

We're conditioned to think of compassion as a fixed personality trait. In truth, it's more like a room in your mind with expandable walls. With committed intentionality and proper guidance, it can go from powder room to great room—with measurable corresponding biological and behavioral changes to boot.

In fact, in the last several decades, specific programs have been developed to help along this expansion. Cognitively-Based Compassion Training (CBCT), Compassionate Mind Training (CMT), and Compassion-Focused Therapy (CFT) are several examples. We can think of these programs as brain and behavior-sculpting regimens for making people more aware, empathic, connected, grateful, and generous. Participants learn and practice techniques to stabilize the mind, deepen self-awareness, cultivate self-compassion, develop equanimity, grow in gratitude, expand affection and empathy, and embody active compassion toward others in both thought and deed.

For centuries, practitioners of compassion—especially in various Buddhist traditions—have taught that training your mind to be more attentive, empathetic, and kind reaps marvelous wellness-enhancing rewards. Siddhartha Gautma (Buddha) said, "a generous heart, kind speech, and a life of service and compassion are the things which renew humanity." Modern-day scientific fields like sociology, psychology, and neuroscience are just catching up to the truth of such teachings. Research programs reveal that people who invest in expanding compassion and self-compassion enjoy an impressive array of health and wellness benefits.

Compassion and Happiness

Ask yourself this: What would happen to your overall mood if, for just one week, you committed to acting compassionately toward someone for 5 minutes daily? Maybe one day you give cash or food to a person experiencing homelessness. Maybe the next day you're extra loving toward your spouse during Saturday morning chores. Would it make a difference in how you felt?

In 2010, Canadian psychologists Myriam Mongrain, Jacqueline M. Chin, and Leah B. Shapira recruited 719 adults and tested exactly this question. In the study, half the participants were instructed to practice compassionate action for 5-15 minutes daily for one week. The other half was told to write daily about an early memory for a week.

Those in the compassion group experienced significant boosts in happiness and self-esteem. The increases in positivity were especially pronounced for those with anxious attachment styles, who tended to ruminate about relationships. What's more, the results lasted. Gains in happiness and self-esteem amongst participants in the compassion group were observable even six months later.[23]

Compassion isn't just fleeting pleasure balm. It's enduring existential nourishment. You know the place deep inside you that cares about the meaning, direction, and legacy of your life? That's what I'm talking about. When we invest intentionally in cultivating kind thoughts and actions towards others, it builds and fortifies our sense of life's purpose. In fact, neuroscientists have found that asking people to empathically imagine themselves in other situations—which is a key aspect of compassion—enhances connectivity in brain areas that mediate our sense of meaning in life.[24]

Thinking, feeling, and acting beyond our own narrow experiences gives our lives greater meaning, coherence, and value. Depressive symptoms (like hopelessness and apathy) lessen as we start to become aware of the supports all around us, and the ways we contribute to others' flourishing. In the words of neuroscientist Barbara Fredrickson (University of North Carolina at Chapel Hill), "—open hearts build lives."[25] Cultivating care for others simply makes us feel good about being alive.

Hold on, you might be thinking. What about all the stuff out there on "compassion fatigue?" Isn't compassion draining and burnout-inducing?

Tania Singer at the Max Planck Institute for Human Cognitive and Brain Sciences in Germany argues that it's empathy, not compassion, that gives rise to burnout and emotional fatigue.[26] In contrast to empathy (merely feeling-with), compassion has a crucial *action* component. It works to accomplish positive change by alleviating someone's suffering. Psychologists have found that experiencing yourself as both connected and effective is powerful medicine. The combination of heartfelt care and active advocacy galvanizes brain areas associated with dopaminergic reward and oxytocin-related affiliative processes.[27] In other words, intentional kindness fires up the same feel-good neurochemicals you'd get eating yummy cupcakes, having great sex, or getting birthday money.

Compassion and Physical Wellness

In addition to its mood-lifting and meaning-deepening aspects, compassion appears to greatly benefit our bodies, too. Research positive psychology founders Martin Seligman and Ed Deiner suggest that connecting meaningfully with other people gives rise to improved overall physical health and speeds disease recovery. Engaging in contemplative compassion practices has been shown to lower systemic inflammation in the body and decrease markers of biological aging.[28] By striving to support and not harm others, our neuroendocrine responses to stress can be lowered, and our ability to heal and grow after traumatic loss can be augmented.[29] Compassion may even lengthen our lifespan. A longitudinal study by Stephanie Brown (Stony Brook University) and Sara Konrath (University of Michigan) found that adults who volunteer regularly out of care and concern for others had a significantly decreased mortality risk.[30]

The neurobiological basis for compassion's physical health benefits is likely rooted in the human attachment system. When we experience compassion (whether given or received), our heart rate slows down. Oxytocin—the "bonding hormone"—is secreted. Brain areas associated with feelings of safety, calm, and joy are activated. In contrast to the toxicity of stress hormones, the neurochemicals linked to safety, attachment, and bonding are profoundly protective of the body's sensitive and complex structures and systems.

So, cultivating compassion appears to supercharge both mental and physical health. What else can it do? Can it make you more personally successful?

Indeed, there's evidence that mindfulness and compassion-based practices *can* increase your verbal fluency, your cognitive flexibility, and the originality of your ideas.[31] These kinds of intellectual aptitudes certainly contribute to success in life and work. However, the greater advantage might be compassion's ability to help you bounce back after difficulties and stay strong in the face of disappointments and challenges.

Self-Compassion and Resilience

One of the most compelling bodies of health-oriented compassion research centers on the link between self-compassion and psychological resilience. As you'll see in later chapters, self-compassion means the ability to recognize our own suffering, perceive it as part of a larger, shared human experience, and intentionally extend kindness to ourselves. By practicing these inward skills of noticing and responding with care to our own pain, we can greatly grow our ability to withstand life's stresses and setbacks, and to get back on track once again.

The practice of self-kindness makes us less vulnerable to being swept away by the whirlwind of emotions many of us contend with daily. A 2017 study illustrates this in a striking way. In the study, a group of Norwegian researchers gave a group of college students a short course in self-compassion. Afterwards, the researchers observed how it impacted the students' ability to self-regulate—in other words, to stay balanced and in command of their thoughts, feelings, and behaviors.[32]

You've likely seen those Brit-inspired t-shirts that say, "Keep Calm and Carry On." Ever met someone who seems to embody and exude that general sentiment? That's the kind of profound equanimity and strength that took root within these students. Compared to a control group, the students that had taken the self-compassion course were better able to be kind to themselves, reduce self-judgment, and redirect negative thoughts. Their overall levels of anxiety and depression fell. They had increases in overall personal growth, in the ability to control impulses, and in their sense of themselves as competent, can-do people. Remarkably, even at a six-month follow up, most of these changes were still in place.

This study is just one of many linking self-compassion with better coping skills in the face of stressors. Self-compassion bolsters our ability to handle hard things ranging from chronic illness[33] to public speaking[34] and much more. Learning to be compassionate with yourself in difficult situations increases your level of emotional grit and mental endurance. It makes you more stable, less self-critical, more flexible, less anxious, more self-controlled, less impulsive, more confident, less self-doubting, more content, and less depressed.

Since life is full of things that threaten to throw us off at every turn, cultivating compassion for ourselves is a major mood protectant and sanity strengthener.

A Rare Commodity

This chapter opened with research suggesting that new companies founded on a high "commitment" model (which prioritizes love and human connection in hiring and management) out-performs companies built on other baseline HR principles. The authors of that well-known study believe this payoff is due to the rarity of such founding principles in people management. "It is a blueprint that runs counter to the conventional wisdom," they conclude.[35]

In other words, *compassion gives organizations a competitive advantage*. Even in today's wellness-obsessed management milieu, it's still relatively difficult to find work cultures that consistently and effectively foster belonging, community, and emotional wellness among employees.

However, when people find these rare jewels, they tend to stay engaged and stick around. In view of the health benefits linked to compassion, it makes sense. When folks find a work culture that makes them feel safe, connected, and part of a shared reality larger than themselves, their brains and bodies tend to thrive.

It turns out that thriving people are the heart and soul of organizational health and success.

Discussion Questions

1. Do you believe compassion is an inherent trait or something that can be cultivated and developed over time? Can you think of examples where individuals have learned to embrace compassion in their professional lives, even if they initially lacked those qualities?

2. What if you committed to act compassionately toward someone for just five minutes daily over the course of one week? How do you think such a commitment would affect your overall mood and well-being? How do you envision it influencing your relationships with others?

3. How do you see the practice of self-compassion contributing to psychological resilience? Can you think of instances in your own life where self-compassion has helped you handle challenging situations and bounce back from setbacks?

Chapter 4
Show Me the Money

Obviously, compassion makes a positive human difference. It creates psychological safety. It helps people heal from trauma. It deepens connection. It instills emotional and physical well-being. Okay, fine. All well and good. I mean, on a purely moral level, the act of fostering human safety, healing, connection, and wellness stands alone in terms of its value and legitimacy. Right?

Yeah, but, c'mon. Let's get real.

If you're reading this, you're likely a businessperson. As a businessperson, you need to know whether there's a *business* case for compassion. Or, as my huge-hearted, whip-smart, and ever-tactful friend Kate (herself a CFO) put it:

> "Okay Andrea. That kinda sounds like woo-woo therapisty kumbaya bullshit. I don't need to give my employees a reason to slack off at work or see me as 'soft.' If you want me to come to your compassionate leadership party, I will, but you're gonna have to show me the money."

If you find yourself thinking similar thoughts, this chapter is for you.

"No Trade-Off Between Care and Progress"

In the Fall of 2019, Pamela Maynard took over as CEO of Avanade—a large, London-based information technology company.[36] Six months into her historic tenure as one of the first and only black female CEOs in tech, the Covid-19 pandemic catapulted the world into an unprecedented and protracted state of emergency. Nine months into Maynard's tenure, the murder of George Floyd ignited widespread outcry against the structures of hate, violence, and injustice that continue to plague our communities. Seventeen months into her tenure, the invasion of Ukraine by Russia propelled waves of social, economic, and political tumult into a world already desperate to catch its breath.

When she started at Avanade, Maynard had been prepared to deal with the ups and downs of adjusting to her new leadership role. The challenges that soon faced her, however, were much more complex than she'd anticipated. What does it mean to be the new CEO of a global tech company *amidst ongoing, pervasive, worldwide catastrophe?* How does one provide executive guidance to tens of thousands of employees and push forward business goals, *while suffering blow after blow of societal trauma?*

There are certain leaders for whom calamity becomes the bedrock of greatness. Maynard is one of them. Her genius was to see that responding compassionately to a worldwide "polycrisis" (to use her term) went hand in hand with growing Avanade's structure, operations, reach, and revenue.

Maynard's unique blend of robust care and badass courage went on full display almost immediately. As the pandemic enveloped everyone in fear and bewilderment, her first move was to prioritize vulnerable connection, unflinching candor, and radical inclusion as she strategized a way forward. Maynard called together her leaders, and said this:

> "Everyone, I don't have the answers. But here's the process I'll be going through to find them. You'll be part of it, and here's how. Know that some balls are going to drop. Know that this will get messy. Know that you'll need to adjust in ways you never thought you'd have to. But at the end, we'll all have more clarity, and we'll have achieved it together."

By admitting that she didn't have the answers, but knew how to map a collective path toward them, Maynard risked revealing her own disorientation and dependence while, at the same time, instilling hope, energy, and confidence. Maynard's transparency instantly made her leaders feel more connected to her, and modeled a way for them to stay connected with their own teams. This sense of togetherness helped galvanize a highly effectual, coordinated response to the crisis.

Another thing Maynard did was to tune into herself—her own instincts and needs—with formidable consistency. As I'll later explain, self-connection and self-compassion are the foundation of compassionate leadership, and Maynard leaned into these with full force. When she needed to identify mentors who could help her tap into the wisdom she knew was inside her, she spent time listening to herself and identifying those people. She became "ruthless" around the time and space boundaries that allowed her to reflect with self-compassionate attention. She learned to note subtle signs (messy desk, short breaths) that she needed a break. In those moments, no matter what was going on, she'd get up and take a walk through the park or sit by the river. She made periodic disconnection and recharge mandatory for herself. By prioritizing her own wellness, Maynard showcased and sanctioned the self-care behaviors her leaders needed to stay grounded, resilient, and effective in the face of maximal stress.

Another crucial move that Maynard made was to implement advocacy-based initiatives that directly met the emotional and humanitarian needs of people in her company and beyond. In the wake of George Floyd's murder—which had a huge emotional impact on her employees during a time when folks were already emotionally exhausted from the pandemic—Maynard created a companywide day of reflection. Employees were told to step away from their work, and intentionally process the pain of racial injustice in whatever ways they found healing. When Russia invaded Ukraine, Maynard tapped into peoples' urge to help. She and her leaders galvanized teams of Avanade workers to take flexible work time to open their homes to refugees, gather food and other supplies, and donate items for those affected by the wartime crisis.

How did Maynard's vulnerability, self-care, and healing/advocacy initiatives affect her organization's financial picture?

Since Avanade hasn't been a publicly traded company since 2008, the answer to that question must be surmised from indirect indicators of business progress. Here are a few.

In the first three years with Maynard as CEO, Avanade:

- Made eight acquisitions. (By way of comparison, the company had made seven acquisitions in eleven years of leadership under former CEO, Adam Warby.)

- Joined the esteemed Microsoft Intelligent Security Association (MISA) alliance.

- Entered the UAE market by opening offices in Abu Dhabi and Dubai.

- Been recognized as the Microsoft Alliance Partner of the Year.

- Built its first US-based engineering center in Tampa, Florida.

- Reached an all-time peak revenue of $2 billion in 2022.

During one of the most traumatizing and chaotic eras in recent history, Avanade exploded with progress and innovation. Business goals were met and exceeded, time and again. The compassionate wisdom inside Pamela Maynard provided a grounding gravitas to her entire leadership team, setting the stage for record-setting company growth. In her words:

"There's no trade-off between care and progress. When we do the trade-off, it's to the detriment of business performance. Care and performance go hand in hand in terms of creating the results we need for clients, employees, and stakeholders."

Avanade's success, under Pamela Maynard's compassionate leadership, is not a fluke. Over the last decade, and especially in the last five to seven years, research on empathy and compassion in the workplace has expanded significantly. It is now possible to get a clear picture of how and why compassionate leadership is so beneficial to an organization's bottom line.

In a word, it's about efficiency. Compassion cuts costs by reducing turnover and boosting productivity. Let's delve into the numbers.

Retention

The pandemic and its aftermath ushered in an era that became known as The Great Resignation. For complex reasons we're still trying to understand, workers began quitting their jobs in droves. A 2021 survey of 326 executives revealed that companies had lost, on average, about 20% of their workforce in just the last six months.[37] At the time of this writing, the so-called "Great Resignation" of the Covid-19 era has perhaps passed, but retention is still a pressing problem. In February 2023 alone, over 400 million workers quit their jobs, and there is now talk of "The Great Gloom."[38]

The cost of turnover varies greatly and is difficult to calculate precisely, but no one disputes that it's expensive. When someone quits, a company must spend money on recruitment, onboarding, and training. The organization also loses money through lowered productivity and increased errors while the new employee learns the ropes. High turnover can also have a negative cultural impact on all employees, lowering morale, productivity, and performance. All of this translates to lost time and revenue, which is why some researchers calculate that each time a business needs to replace an employee, it costs 6 to 9 months' salary. Others say the cost of replacement is more like one to two times an employee's annual salary.[39] Whatever the exact cost, high turnover is a significant financial drain on any company.

When it comes to compassion and retention, research over the last several years strongly suggests that two things are true. First, *less compassion means more turnover.* According to Gallup, employees who don't feel their manager cares about them as a person are 37% more likely to resign.[40] Cengage found that 89% of workers who had recently left their job, or were planning to leave, felt burnt out and unsupported.[41] The consulting firm EY reported that 54% of employees say they've left a previous job because their boss wasn't empathetic to their struggles at work or in their personal lives.[42] According to research conducted by BusinessSolver, 82% of employees say they would leave their position to work for a more empathetic organization.[43]

The second truth is that *more compassion means less turnover.* EY reports that 79% of workers feel that empathetic leadership in the workplace decreases turnover.[44] The research and consulting group Catalyst, which focuses on women in the workplace, found that 62% of women of color said they were unlikely to think of leaving their companies when they felt their life circumstances were respected and valued by their companies.[45] Research by Rasmus Hougaard and Jacqueline Carter reveals that highly compassionate leaders *themselves* have 200% lower intention to resign.[46] Also, employees who experience their manager as compassionate have a 36% higher commitment to the organization.[47]

Right now, top talent is looking to join and stay at companies who create everyday conditions where people feel seen, known, and advocated for. Working people—especially those belonging to younger generations like Millennials and Gen Z—are keenly aware that they spend the best hours of each day, and the best years of their lives, at work. So they want it to be a place where they feel good—where they're supported, connected, and cared for, especially by their managers. In fact, a recent survey by QuestionPro revealed that only 1 in 5 employees say they *don't* want to have a better personal and professional connection with their manager.[48]

It is simply the case that when it comes to attracting and retaining the talented people who make an organization great, compassionate leadership is no longer a 'nice-to-have'. It's essential.

Engagement

Recently, a local SHRM (Society for Human Resources Management) chapter in my home state gathered to commemorate 50 years in existence. I was honored to provide a keynote address at this celebratory assembly of leaders in the field of Human Resources. At one point in my talk, I asked the 69-member strong audience to participate in a live poll. The question was: "In the last year, how problematic has "quiet quitting" been in your organization?"

I knew numbers would be high, but I admit that even I was shocked when only *four* HR directors responded, "not problematic." A whopping 94% of those present had struggled to some degree with the problem of people coming to work but doing the barest of minimums.

The crises of 2020 and beyond have brought employee engagement to record lows, and the problem isn't letting up. As I explained in previous chapters, as a trauma-informed therapist, I'm convinced the pervasive challenge of employee disengagement is a manifestation of collective human pain and trauma. We're people living in a time of unprecedented volatility, uncertainty, complexity, and ambiguity. We're wounded and we don't feel safe. We're out of bandwidth and we're in survival mode. It makes sense, then, that we instinctually pull back and conserve energy in every domain possible—including work. It's what our nervous systems have evolved to do.

And it's been expensive. According to a study by *The Conference Board*,[49] a global nonprofit business think tank, quiet quitting has cost U.S. businesses 450 to 500 billion dollars annually.

In this context, compassionate leaders and organizational cultures are crucial. When people spend their days in a compassionate work environment—when they feel connection and active care, especially from their manager—they are more present, interested, innovative, and efficient. Compassionate work cultures are directly linked to lower employee absenteeism and emotional exhaustion.[50] Neuroimaging research even shows that people's brains respond more positively to leaders who demonstrate compassion.[51]

The statistics linking caring leadership and employee engagement are compelling. Seventy-six percent of workers who feel their manager is empathetic to their struggles are highly engaged at work. This is compared with only thirty-two percent who experienced a lack of empathy from their manager.[52] Eighty-seven percent of employees agree that mutual empathy between leaders and employees increases efficiency, creativity, and innovation.[53] Eighty-five percent of employees report that caring, connected leadership in the workplace increases productivity.[54] And, by raising the level of managerial compassion in the workplace, employers can expect a forty-one percent drop in worker absenteeism.[55]

In an environment of genuine connection, care, and support, people simply get more done. This renewed vitality and interest isn't a conscious choice. It isn't as if an employee says, "Gee, Boss asked whether my kid's new therapist is working out; think I'll work extra hard on this spreadsheet today." No, the reengagement happens at preconscious levels. When a traumatized nervous system perceives that it's in a context of true human care, it starts to deactivate the threat response system that's caused it to go into freeze mode. Cognitive resources slowly get redirected to executive (prefrontal) functioning. In other words, the person starts to exit survival mode because they sense they belong. Belonging brings psychological safety, and psychological safety gives the mind permission to stop protecting and return to a more alert, interested, and motivated state of flow.

Who Would've Thought?

Amid the Covid-19 pandemic and all the chaos it brought to business, Clinton Goodwin, COO of Fujitsu General, decided that everyone in his company needed to cultivate more compassion within themselves and between others. So all Fujitsu employees underwent a program that educated them on skills like stilling the mind, engaging the heart, being patient, being vulnerable, listening and tending, and asking excellent questions of each other.

It has revolutionized the emotional tenor of the organization, fueling personal growth and relationship development at all levels of leadership.

Its effect on the bottom line? When Goodwin was asked during a panel discussion to describe the effects of that investment, he said this:

> "Our business outcomes are far better than they've ever been. We're kicking more goals by being vulnerable and compassionate; who would've thought? It's really worked for us as a business."[56]

Wise leaders today understand the powerful financial payoff of working to build a culture of compassion within their organization. How do you do that? What are the steps, and where do you start? Those are the excellent questions to which we'll now turn.

Discussion Questions

1. How do you perceive the impact of genuine connection, care, and support on employee productivity and engagement? Can you think of examples where individuals have experienced a shift from a survival mode mentality to a state of flow and increased motivation due to a sense of belonging and psychological safety?

2. In the context of leadership development, how can leaders create an environment that fosters genuine connection and psychological safety, thereby enabling employees to tap into their full cognitive resources and reach a state of heightened productivity and engagement?

Part II
Self-Compassion

CHAPTER 5
MEET YOUR INNER CRITIC

Compassion for others begins with kindness to ourselves.
— Pema Chödrön

I devoted my twenties and most of my thirties to climbing the ranks of academia. My goal was to rise from my humble origins as an undergrad at a small midwestern college, to a tenure-track professorship at a top research university on the east coast. By the time I was 35, I had met my goal.

How did I do it? Yeah, I was passionate. Yeah, I was dedicated. Yeah, I was hard-working. The unknown x-factor that no one saw was that my success depended, heavily and consistently, on the shrill and unrelenting voice of my inner self-critic.

I recall giving a presentation on neuroscience and spirituality at Princeton. It went well overall. People were interested in the work I was doing on ancient spiritual practices and modern-day brain science. At the end of the Q&A, however, a gray-bearded scholar stood up. He'd been sitting in the front row, and he had a scowl on his face throughout most of my talk. He asked me if I'd looked closely at the *Latin* of the spiritual text I'd been referencing because, in the original Latin, it seems to indicate that [*blah blah blah, I won't bore you with details, but he went on to severely challenge my work based on the fact that I'd been relying mainly on an English translation*].

My inner critic sprang into action. *"Why didn't you look at the original medieval Latin text? Because you don't know medieval Latin, now, do you? You're so lazy, such a dabbler, a complete imposter, unworthy of real scholarly respect. If you want to do this work, you better not just learn neuroscience, you better get your ass in gear and teach yourself medieval Latin, too."* Goaded by the whip of this

45

inner oppressor, I added to my already impossibly full plate of teaching, committee work, student mentoring, scientific research, and spiritual investigation: **LEARN LATIN. NOW.**

You might guess what happened. Yep. I burned out. When I was 36, I walked away from my dream job at Boston University, and never returned to full-time academia. Of course, there were multiple factors that went into this decision. Now that I know about the devastating effects of constant inner criticism, and the amazing benefits of a different approach—a self-compassionate approach—I sometimes wonder what would've happened if I'd managed to bestow kindness, understanding, empathy, and grace upon myself. Instead of, you know, bludgeoning myself along with the constant message that I wasn't enough, and probably never would be.

The Tyranny of the Inner Critic

Turns out, it wasn't just me. Research by Dr. Karol M. Wasylyshyn shows that many leaders rely heavily on self-criticism to keep them focused and motivated.[57] In the words of one business leader, "I was [simply] *unable* to see that there were things I was doing well. I could brush off any praise and move [with swift harshness] to where I needed to improve."[58] Sound familiar?

As children, most of us received correction or criticism when we didn't meet adults' expectations. To an extent, it's healthy to internalize this—to have an inner part of ourselves that notices when we're missing the mark in some way and guides us to change course. Leaders, especially, *should* have high standards for themselves, and *should* have a reliable ability to self-correct when needed.

Even so, holding high standards and aspirations can sometimes morph into what researchers call "maladaptive perfectionism."[59] The main marker of this is high levels of self-criticism, even shame, but also:

- Difficulty recovering from mistakes or setbacks
- A tendency to avoid situations in which one may appear incompetent
- A tendency to approach problems rigidly
- A tendency to procrastinate
- A tendency to work in isolation, and resist seeking support
- Problems with anxiety and depression
- A kneejerk instinct to protect one's ego at all costs
- Inability to "unplug" from work
- A tendency toward burnout
- A tendency to be highly critical of others

Self-castigation. Rigidity. Procrastination. Isolation. Anxiousness. Defensiveness. If *resilience* is the ability to recover swiftly and gracefully from mistakes and difficulties, then maladaptive perfectionism is pretty much the total opposite of resilience. In fact, chronically stressing about not measuring up can lead to mental and physical health problems, and can even speed up biological aging.[60]

When you're a maladaptively perfectionistic leader, it can end up affecting your whole team. *Everyone* ends up feeling stressed and inadequate. Ever been around someone who exudes criticality, both for themselves and others? It makes you feel like you don't measure up before you've even begun.

The Neuroendocrinology of Self-Criticism

Let's consider for a minute what happens inside our bodies when we're berating ourselves. The anterior cingulate cortex is the part of the brain responsible for error detection, cognitive conflict monitoring, social rejection, fear, anxiety, and relationship loss. Along with the amygdala, the anterior cingulate is part of the human *threat detection system*. This system is ancient and primal. It evolved to keep us safe, and so gets activated whenever we sense peril, *including social peril.* Stress hormones like cortisol get pumped into our body, preparing us to fight, flee, or freeze.

Chronic self-criticism means we're imperiling *ourselves* with inner violence and rejection. Our brains can't tell that we're the ones doing the castigating; neuroimaging studies show that harsh criticism, whether it comes from ourselves or another, puts our brain and body in "threat mode." This does significant damage over time. Research shows that a chronically activated threat detection system can wreak havoc on both physical and emotional health.[61]

Why Are We Self-Critical?

Self-criticism is very hard on our mental health. It's associated with higher rates of not only anxiety and depression, but also non-suicidal self-injury, like substance misuse, eating disorders, and other destructive behaviors.

If it's so hard on us, why do we keep beating ourselves up? Let's explore some of the underlying reasons we tend to be so self-critical.

Reason #1: "Never Enough" Culture. Brené Brown calls this "scarcity culture." Everywhere, there's this subtle or not-so-subtle message: If you want to be respected and valued, you'd better be more successful, more certain, more extraordinary. You must be thinner, smarter, healthier, stronger, wealthier, funnier. Between the supermodel ads, and the Instagram pics of the *perfect* neighbor's *perfect* family on their *perfect* vacation, we're left with: *"I'm sub-par and I know it."*

Reason #2: We need Social Acceptance. We humans are super scared of rejection. We're hyper-vigilant about anything that could bring reproach from others. It's as if you say to yourself, "I know, I know, I suck. I'm going to put myself down before you do. Then maybe you'll not judge me so harshly." The dog that goes belly up still gets fed, after all.

Reason #3: We Grew Up Hearing Criticism. Maybe you grew up with a parent who voiced a lot of their own self-criticism to cope with life. Or perhaps they doled out regular reproach toward you for not measuring up. If so, the negative running commentary in your head is likely a reflection of what was impressed on you as a youngster. Early on, you learned that harsh disapproval is a normal way of relating to yourself and others.

Reason #4: We Desire Power and Control. Sometimes our lives feel so out of control that the feeling of beating ourselves up brings some relief. At least we can be powerful somewhere. At least we can be superior to *something*—namely, the parts of ourselves we don't like. There can be a sick pleasure we can get from self-flagellation. It comes from feeling in-control, when everywhere else we're getting the message that we're powerless.

Reason #5: We Have Unmet Needs. Think about how toddlers get when they've not had enough sleep, or when they're hungry, or when their environment is too overstimulating, or when another kid didn't share. They scream and kick; they flail and rage. As adults, it's not socially acceptable to throw a fit! Yet, that energy is still there because we have unmet needs. So, we turn it all inward, and rage against ourselves.

Reason #6: We're on Autopilot. Negative emotions are often our default, and they have a way of taking over and affecting everything. There's a very unfortunate but all-too-human mental habit called "rumination," which neuroscientists have linked to a brain area called the default mode network. This brain system keeps us chewing on negative thoughts, like a cow on cud. To everyone else, we may appear to be getting along fine, but in the background is a running commentary of anxious, half-formed, thoughts that we can't seem to step outside of.

Whatever the underlying reasons for self-criticism, healing from it is crucial if you want to be a more compassionate, wise, and resilient person and people leader. Let's talk about how to do that.

Discussion Questions

1. Markers of maladaptive perfectionism can often be concealed by outward appearances of being hardworking and successful. Which aspects of maladaptive perfectionism resonated with you personally? Can you share any experiences or examples that demonstrate these markers in your own life?

2. How do societal expectations and the fear of social rejection contribute to self-criticism?

3. Can you relate to any of the reasons mentioned for self-criticism in your own life? How have these factors influenced your self-perception and interactions with others?

CHAPTER 6
INTRODUCING SELF-COMPASSION

Despite the downsides of being hard on yourself, many leaders are deeply attached to their inner critic. I know I was convinced my inner critic was responsible for my success. She held a whip in her hand that was called DYSTUOE (Don't You Screw This Up, Or Else), and it was my main motivator.

Because my field was spirituality and neuropsychology, I was vaguely aware of the groundbreaking research being done on self-compassion by a young researcher at the University of Texas Austin named Kristin Neff. According to Neff, self-compassion means "loving, connected presence"[62] to one's own self. It means strengthening your inner ally, and weakening your inner saboteur.

At the height of my academic success, I blindly assumed that if I took a self-compassionate stance toward myself—if I actually *did* this—I'd become lazy, incompetent, and unproductive. My inner slacker would take over, and I'd fail at life. I just knew it, knew it. So I basically ignored this whole field of research and focused on other, more important things. (Like medieval Latin.)

As we'll soon see, I was completely mistaken in my assumptions. Before we explore the incredible benefits of self-compassion for health, wholeness, and resilience, let's take a closer look at the three main elements of self-compassion.

Mindfulness
The first step in becoming self-compassionate is noticing what's going on inside. Many of us can't tell when we're in emotional distress. We just suddenly find ourselves yelling or sobbing or binging or isolating or something else we don't want to be doing. What we need is *mindfulness*: attentive, non-judgmental, accepting curiosity about our own present-moment experience.

People sometimes think that to be mindful, you need to meditate. Meditation is incredibly important and helpful, but it's not always practical. You can be mindful anytime, anywhere.

First, *quiet yourself.* Find a way to still your mind. Soothing your body is the best way to begin to settle down your mind. Here are a few ideas.

- Find a place that's literally quiet, or at least quiet*er* (I have a young child, so yes, sometimes it's the bathroom, with shower and fan both on.)

- Take two or three deep breaths. Try to focus on how the air feels coming in and out of your body. I like to "watch" the air come in through my nostrils, and out through my lips.

- Rub your own arms in a soothing motion, or put your hand gently on your heart or stomach.

- Press your thumb to the space between your eyes and tell yourself quietly, "Ssshhh. Be still."

The second key to mindfulness is to *be curious.* When I was in graduate school, I had a professor who taught a class where lots of controversial topics were explored. Whenever the discussion got complicated, he'd turn to whoever was talking and say, "Huh. Can you say more about that?" Ever since then, this is what curiosity sounds like to me—it's a gentle, "*Huh.*" It's the sound of openness, interest, attentiveness, and acceptance. It says, "You're safe. I'm here. I'm listening. I won't judge you. Say more."

Each of us has a whole host of characters within us. When we get curious about them, they come out of the woodwork. The anxious one might need to tell you about her fear of an upcoming mid-year review. The lonely one might tell you she's worried she'll never find a friend she can trust. The annoyed one might tell you she's still stinging from that passive-aggressive cashier at IKEA.

The tempted one might tell you she really, *really* wants brownies right now and is exhausted from resisting. It could be anything.

The thing that happens when we become curious about ourselves is that we suddenly can *see* our feelings instead of being wrapped up in them. We're grounded down (*whomp!*) in our still place, *observing* what's going on instead of being *swept away* by it. Our suffering becomes a part of us rather than the whole, and we get to choose how we relate to that suffering. Revolutionary.

Common Humanity

The second crucial element of self-compassion is seeing and accepting that everyone messes up—everyone suffers. We're only human after all. When you start to see mistakes and hurts as just a normal part of life, they lose their power to make you feel alone and ashamed. Let's be honest; when things are hard, it's often the loneliness and shame that hurt the most.

One day, when I was in my mid-twenties, I went into work on a Monday feeling awful about myself. I had seriously overeaten that previous weekend. My clothes felt tight, my face and fingers felt bloated, and I felt sluggish and headachy. The worst part of it was the inward shaming. The general message I was sending myself was, "You're disgusting and sad. I won't accept you until you've been 'good' with your diet/exercise for at least three days. So keep your head down, eat your salads, and run your ass off."

A lovely co-worker, who'd become a good friend, noticed I wasn't quite myself, and she checked in with me. I told her I was feeling gross because I'd not made the best eating decisions that weekend. Holly was a young, beautiful gal—peaceful in spirit and strong in presence. I assumed she'd never experienced anything like what I was going through. She surprised me by saying, "Oh, yeah, it wasn't a great weekend for me that way, too. I downed an entire mega-size bag of potato chips last night."

I hid it well, but I was surprised. I mean, really? This seemingly perfect co-worker had stuffed her face with Frito-Lays? Last night?

"Yeah." She sighed, in a light-hearted way. "Who *hasn't* pigged out on junk food and then regretted it? I've realized it's just something that sometimes happens, and I try not to beat myself up. It's not the end of the world. I'll feel better tomorrow. So will you!"

For someone who'd been used to self-flagellation in this sensitive area of food, weight, and body image, I was kind of floored by what Holly modeled for me. That conversation became a step in a new journey for me: learning to relate to my body with kindness, especially when I'd overindulged.

My point is that when we feel isolated in our pain, it intensifies the feelings of deficiency and amps up the self-criticism. We feel like we're the only ones going through this. We're not. It's completely normal to make bad decisions. It's completely normal for junky things to happen. It's completely normal to fail to live up to our best intentions.

If you struggle with perfectionism or have a competitive edge, it can be especially difficult to see that hardship and failure are inevitable, are part of our common humanity. The inner compulsive achiever can be a tough one to live with: the stress and anxiety about getting things just right, the dissatisfaction or devastation when they don't. For perfectionists, self-compassion involves not just accepting, but coming to appreciate, the gift of struggle.[63] To be a living person means to be in motion; everything is in flux and you're just *going to* experience highs and lows. That's part of what makes life beautiful and interesting. So you can stop judging yourself so harshly because we're all in this together.

Self-Kindness

The third element of self-compassion is simply learning to be kind, gentle, and tender toward ourselves, especially when we're in a tough moment. Many of us suffer from regular self-criticism and self-judgment. Many of us live within the madness of a never-ending inner war.

Internal Family Systems Theory[64] teaches that, at any given moment, there's a whole cast of active characters within us. When we're in pain, our inner community (or family) is especially complicated. In this case, it's important to let *all* the characters be welcomed, seen, and heard. There's the one who's feeling awful because of some hard or hurtful thing. Often, there's the one who's being harsh, even cruel, with self-critical inner talk and/or self-sabotaging behaviors. However, inside each of us is also the kind, understanding one—the unconditionally compassionate one. The one who calmly notices what's going on and, like a loving parent toward a dysregulated child, says things like:

- "This is hard right now. Let me take care of you."
- "Oh, my dear. I'm sorry you're going through this."
- I know, I know. This moment is difficult, isn't it. Sshhhhh. I've got you."
- "I am here."

I believe this wise and caring part of us is very special, even sacred. Connecting with your inner advocate can be a profoundly meaningful experience, opening whole new vistas of healing and well-being.

The Benefits of Self-Compassion

Unexamined beliefs so often lead us astray. The younger me, who assumed self-compassion would make me self-indulgent and unmotivated, was just plain *wrong*. Research on the benefits of self-compassion has been accruing for several decades. Thousands of studies link self-compassion to high personal standards, high motivation to succeed, greater levels of self-initiative, and greater self-confidence.

Self-compassion doesn't make you a slacker. Rather, it takes the time and energy you were using to worriedly beat yourself up, and directs it toward helping you achieve your goals with peace and happiness.

Let's look at some of the other great things to which studies link self-compassion:

- Higher job satisfaction
- Healthier habits, like exercise and nutritious eating
- Greater levels of self-confidence and personal initiative
- Lowered depression, anxiety, and feelings of shame
- Less fear of failure, and less rumination when things go wrong
- Reduced interpersonal conflict and avoidance
- Higher emotional intelligence
- Increased agreeableness, extroversion, conscientiousness
- Greater likelihood of being compassionate and forgiving toward others
- Greater curiosity and eagerness to explore

This is just a short list of benefits. Much more could be said. Self-compassion has even been linked to better sleep,[65] and increased ability to relate to people across differences.[66]

Self-Compassion and Resilience

When it comes to resilience—strength and stability amid stress and suffering—self-compassion is especially impressive.

Case in point. In 2014, researchers at the University of Colorado Boulder took 105 undergraduates and measured their stress response while they were asked to deliver an impromptu speech and perform mental arithmetic in front of an audience.[67] (Just a *little bit* nerve-racking, right?) A third of the students had done a brief self-compassion training a few days beforehand, where they learned to meditate with mantras like "May I be happy; may I be at ease; may I know that my joys and struggles are shared by others." Another third had listened to recordings of a psychology textbook, and another third hadn't done anything different at all beforehand.

The stress responses of the self-compassion group (measured through heart rate, certain stress chemicals in saliva, and self-reported feelings of anxiety) were far lower than that of the other two. It wasn't that the self-compassion students weren't experiencing distress. Cortisol, which the body produces in situations of unpredictability, was present in *all* of the students' saliva during the ordeal. Rather, the students in the self-compassion group were better able to *respond to* and *recover from* the ordeal and the distress it caused them. They used their newly acquired self-compassion skills to notice their suffering, remember that suffering is a part of human life, and give themselves a hefty dose of kindness during a tough moment. Their bodies responded by activating the parasympathetic system—the one responsible for soothing us and calming us down.

Leadership is stressful. The difference between good and great leaders may lie in the ability to withstand hardship, recover quickly, and move forward with gratitude for another lesson learned. That's what resilience is all about, and it's exactly what the students in the experimental group accomplished. They were able to reinterpret, reevaluate, recalibrate, and refuel in the wake of adversity and challenge.

Self-compassion helps make resilience possible. It trains us to re-set inwardly, to find our emotional footing again after we've been thrown for a loop. Study after study has demonstrated it. However, since self-criticism is often so deeply engrained, it takes strategic intentionality to create newer, kinder, more resilient ways of relating to yourself. Luckily, the next chapter offers inspiration and guidance for just that.

Discussion Questions

1. Practice and reflect on the mindfulness exercise described in the chapter. Share your experience of engaging in the practice and its impact on your state of mind and well-being.

2. Before engaging in the mindfulness practice, how would you describe your emotional state or overall sense of being? After practicing mindfulness, did you notice any changes in how you felt? What specific differences or shifts did you observe?

3. What is it like to speak kindly to yourself? Does it initially feel unfamiliar, uncomfortable, or like a novel idea? How do you perceive the importance of self-compassionate self-talk in promoting well-being and resilience?

CHAPTER 7
DOING SELF-COMPASSION

Self-compassion is about experiencing your own mind as a safety zone. You learn to trust that, at least here, you won't be neglected or berated. There's an "adult in the room" who knows how to lovingly take charge and bring stability again. Your own self becomes the place where you will be cared for. You become a refuge for yourself.

What does this look like in real life? Especially life at work?

To illustrate, let me tell you a true story about my friend, Rushmie Nofsinger. Rushmie is VP of Corporate Affairs at Scholar Rock, a Boston-based biopharmaceutical company. Several years ago, however, she headed up PR at a different company—one where the executives intentionally encouraged a culture of rivalry because they believed it would drive performance—and it worked, to a certain extent. It also tended to fuel anger, fear, and insecurity.

At the time, there was another high-performing woman who headed up a different department. Rushmie was often compared to her. Both reported to the same person, both were powerhouses of talent, and both happened to be Indian women.

Then one day, a rumor started rumbling. A possible re-org—a re-org in which Rushmie might begin *reporting up* to this other woman.

Inwardly, Rushmie battled feelings of anger, indignance, and insecurity. Why should *she* report up to this other person who'd always been her equal?

After work, consumed with frustration, hips swinging and proverbial guns blazing, she got in her car and zoomed off to a place she knew could handle everything she was feeling. A place that provides solace amidst all manner of chaos. A place that, in fact, solves pretty much every problem.

Target.

As she jimmied her car into a parking spot and slam-shifted it into park, Rushmie found she couldn't go in. She was too upset. Then, something happened while she was sitting in her car.

Rushmie took a deep breath and found she was able to step outside of her anger and see it for what it was: a cover for pain. The toxic rivalry had pitted Rushmie against someone who was in no way her actual adversary. This other talented Indian businesswoman *should* be her friend, her collaborator, her sister in solidary—and Rushmie should be hers. Both had been hurt by the company's pervasive culture of competition.

After seeing her pain for what it was, Rushmie calmed a bit. Then she realized something else. The type of anger and hurt she was experiencing is something people suffer from when they've been subtly manipulated by toxic systems—when they've been sneakily swayed into seeing peers, who could be strong supporters, as ominous threats. It's one of the ways in which unhealthy systems function to keep people down—especially people in under-represented groups.

So, still sitting in her car in the Target parking lot, Rushmie made an incredibly courageous decision. She chose to side with compassion and empowerment—both for herself, and for her colleague:

> *"I realized I had a choice. Either I could work against this person as a force that continually opposed her. Or, if I had to report up to her, I could do the very best damn job possible, so that as her boat rose, mine would too. I realized that, for her to win, I didn't have to lose. We rise by lifting each other up."*

As it turned out, Rushmie didn't end up reporting to this person, but the choice she made for kindness and mutual empowerment impacted both women in positive ways. Although they're no longer at the same company, they've both enjoyed tremendous success in their careers. To this day, they are very close friends, confidantes, collaborators, and cheerleaders of one another.

Summoning the Inner Parent

When we face challenges of any kind, self-sabotaging thoughts are one of the main things that keep us down. When she got wind of the possible re-org, Rushmie was pissed off. When we're pissed off, it's often because we're down on ourselves. Underneath Rushmie's anger were feelings of inadequacy and self-doubt.

In these moments, we need our wise inner parent to come and help keep us from spiraling.

On my read, Rushmie's wise inner parent is exactly who showed up as she sat fuming in the Target parking lot. *"Ssshhhh, honey. Breathe. You're angry. What else are you feeling? Oh, you're hurt? Of course you are, that makes perfect sense."* Once her inner parent helped her calm down and see what was going on, the next thing was to realize she wasn't alone. These feelings of anger, inadequacy, and sadness are something that *many* people feel. Experiencing them is part of what it means to be human, especially in toxic work cultures.

The last thing her inner parent helped her do was to choose kindness and empowerment. I imagine this wise inner parent saying to Rushmie:

> *"You don't have to stay in this self-sabotaging state of frustration. This isn't a zero-sum game, sweetheart. You can believe in you—you can see yourself as worthy and capable of great things. AND? You can believe in her—you can see her as worthy of great things, too. Be brave. Choose to side with yourself, and side with her, too."*

Rushmie's inner parent was leading her through the three steps of mindful self-compassion: First, notice you're in pain. Second, remember that pain is part of being human. Third, choose kindness and care toward yourself and others.

I promise that if you put those three steps into action, your boat will rise, and others' will, too.

Your Self-Compassion Toolkit

Self-compassion is a skill that must be practiced. It can feel strange at first, but becomes more natural with time. Here are five tools for strengthening your self-compassion muscles and fortifying your inner refuge—especially when you're stuck within emotional negativity.

Heed the Call of Mindfulness. When you're ruminating or overidentified with your emotions, freeing yourself can feel a little bit impossible. If you can attune yourself inwardly, even a little bit, you may hear a still, small voice saying, *"This isn't all there is. This isn't all you are. There's another way."* This voice—whether you call it conscience, spirit, God, or simply your wisest self—is asking you to start with mindfulness. To start with simply observing that, yes, you're experiencing something uncomfortable. Here's the magic: As soon as you *notice* you're suffering, you immediately become a bit more *distant* from it, and that in itself is a great relief. So next time you're in the thick of it, try to fix your inward ears on the call of mindfulness. It's the first step on the way to peace.

Feel All, Greet All. Self-compassion refuses to push away negative emotions, however hard they are to face. I love the Marcel Proust quote, "We are healed from suffering only by experiencing it to the full."[68] Once you've heeded the call of mindfulness, and find you're able to observe your suffering (huge step in itself), try to greet your negative emotions by name (e.g., "Hello grief." "Hello rage."). If you can't get a handle on what it is you're feeling, which is totally normal, then greet it by the name, "Impulse." You can inwardly say, "Oh, hello, Impulse." That might seem weird until you remember that all negative emotions that threaten to carry us away are, in some sense, impulses. They're compulsions that bubble up from the more primitive parts of our brains. Never judge yourself for having negative emotions and/or impulses. Greet them without indignation, for these things are simply a part of the human journey.

Downregulate. Now it's time to dole out some self-kindness and help yourself go from overstimulated to calm. In scientific speak, from a state in which your sympathetic nervous system is dominant, to one where your parasympathetic nervous system is dominant.[69] Ask what you can do to put your body at rest. It's always good to start with the breath, so let your first step be a deep inhale through your nose, hold for the count of four, and a long, slow, deep release through the mouth. Beyond that, you can try several things. First, rocking your fears to sleep. Put your hand on your chest, begin to gently rock your body, as a loving mother would rock an overwrought child to sleep. Alternatively, try lying on the floor and doing some calming body postures. If you're a yogi, maybe it's child's pose or downward dog. Something that sometimes works for me is lying down and putting my feet up on the wall for five minutes. Also, if you're socially sensitive, try limiting your errands that day, or resting in a dark quiet room for ten minutes. A few final downregulation strategies include napping, taking a walk, taking a bath, watching some comedy, petting your dog, or looking out the window and picking just one leaf or twig to observe, as it shimmers in the breeze.

Speak Soothing Words. The practice of changing your self-talk is a crucial strategy for meeting difficult emotions with self-compassion, and for becoming more emotionally resilient. I urge you to play around with different ways of talking to yourself. You can either do it inwardly or out loud. (I often do it when I'm alone in the car.) "Sweet girl, I know, I know." "This is hard." "I get it, I understand, it makes so much sense that you feel that way." "It's OK, you're OK." "You are a strong, competent person." "Look, you're doing it. You've got this." The point is that you've got to find the words that will work for *you*. Even try to find a pet name by which to call yourself—something that sounds loving and authentic, like being addressed by someone who knows and loves you through and through.

Try the self-compassion break. This is a great one-minute "shortcut" to use when you're feeling overwhelmed with difficult emotions at work.[70] The next time you notice you're in a tough moment, whether big or small, try this. First, offer yourself a soothing touch. Perhaps put a hand over your heart, or belly, or cheek. Then, in the gentlest of tones, say the following three things to yourself:

- *"This is a moment of suffering."* (Or an equivalent, like, *"This is so hard."*)

- *"Suffering is a part of life."* (Or an equivalent, like, *"But it isn't abnormal."*)

- *"May I be kind to myself."* (Or an equivalent, like, *"I'll be good to myself."*)

This this three-part mantra can become a wonderful tool for you in daily life as you seek to grow in self-compassion.

Finding Stillness

When we're deeply unsettled by self-criticism or other difficult emotions, stillness is what we most seek. Just as far below the choppy foamy ocean waves there is a deep yet vibrant quiescence, I believe that for each person, stillness is always there as a possibility, beneath the clamorous crashing of daily fears and desires. It's less a matter of adding stillness into your life, and more a matter of removing obstacles to the peace that's already there, deep within you.

Learning to settle yourself within those depths is always a journey. In classical Daoist spirituality, getting to the place of clarity and stillness (*qingjing*) involves five meditative stages, or moments: major agitation, minor agitation, equilibrium of agitation, and stillness, minor stillness, and major stillness. It's as if you are sinking, down, down—deeper toward the wisdom deep inside.

There's an eighth century Daoist text that talks about this journey in such beautiful terms. The meditator, on his way to stillness, first observes ten thousand beings arising and multiplying; they are everywhere. Then, one by one, he watches as each being returns to its Source:

Returning to the Source is called stillness;
This means returning to life-destiny.
Returning to life-destiny is called constancy;
Knowing constancy is called illumination.[71]

You were never meant to suffer within the clamorous push and pull of anxious, strident, self-condemning thoughts. They are corrosive to your leadership journey, and they threaten the joyful flourishing of what poet Mary Oliver calls "your one wild and precious life." So, journey onward and ever deeper. Let self-compassion be your guide as you sink down toward the stillness, strength, and lovingkindness within.

Discussion Questions

1. Did you find any parts of Rushmie's story relatable or personally resonant? Can you think of any specific stories or experiences from your own life that came to mind while reading?

2. Review the self-compassion toolkit practices mentioned. Which ones stood out to you as particularly appealing or attractive? Why does that practice resonate with you?

3. Moments of stillness can be valuable for self-reflection and cultivating self-compassion. When do you personally experience moments of stillness in your life? How do these moments contribute to your overall well-being and ability to show compassion to yourself and others?

Part III
Awareness

CHAPTER 8
HERE AND NOW

In 2012, I was living in the bustling city of Chicago, finishing up my Ph.D. I was stressed to the max—teaching part-time, trying to finish my dissertation, and applying for jobs. Also, my husband and I were struggling with infertility. Also, I was attempting to kick several intertwined addictions that had cropped up during my studies.

It was a lot to shoulder.

To manage the stress, I'd begun doing mindfulness meditation every day for twenty minutes. After my morning run or bike ride, I'd sit in the lotus position on my cramped but cozy hardwood living room floor. I'd close my eyes and turn my focus inward—zeroing in on the cool stream of air as it entered my nostrils, and the warm exhale that flowed through my mouth. I pictured my breath as a ribbon of tiny multicolored particles that entered and exited my body in a beautiful thread of luminous movement. My job was to simply watch it flow through me. When thoughts would crowd, I'd calmly notice them and then dismiss them, returning my focus to the ribbon. Over, and over, and over again.

One day, perhaps a month into my mindfulness regimen, I was walking on a sidewalk along North Sheridan Road. Suddenly, the worries I'd been nursing around my dissertation melted away, and the world seemed to spring and shimmer into life. In what felt like a slow-motion sequence, I began to experience in granular detail *each and every step* I was taking. I *felt* my heel touch the concrete. As my legs pushed my body forward, I *felt* the pressure of gravity roll forward onto the ball of my foot, and then my toes, before letting go into the next step with the opposite foot. I looked up, and now I *smelled* the scent of doughnuts coming from the nearby bakery. I *saw* the woman with the red scarf as she walked toward me. I *heard* the pigeons cooing and flapping in a courtyard to my left. I remember feeling overwhelmed with the joy of being awake and alive to take all this in.

The simple act of walking down the street had become something of a miracle.

Mindful awareness has the potential to transform your life, because it opens a way for you to actually *live* your life. You begin to *experience* your moment-to-moment existence, rather than numbing, worrying, scheming, or fantasizing your way through it. As Buddhist monk and teacher Thich Nhat Hanh says, the "address" of happiness is "here and now."

The present moment is the only moment in which you can feel, decide, love, and lead. It is all there is.

As I walked down the sidewalk that day, I realized that mindfulness meditation was helping me to make the "here and now" my permanent home. I was truly aware, truly present. I couldn't believe how good it felt.

I want this happiness to come to you, too. Not simply because I want you to be happy—*although that is very true*—but also because it is impossible to be a compassionate leader without a baseline of calm, observant, *awareness*—both to self and other. People trust and follow leaders whose very presence exudes a strong, centered, *thereness.* Such a bearing assures them they are safe and connected—that they're cared for, and they belong.

Awareness is the secret ingredient to embodying this type of authentic presence.

Awareness begins with mindful attention to your own experience of the present moment. If you're unfocused within— disconnected from yourself, and/or battling an inward conflict— you cannot be present, poised, confident, and connected to (and with) others. Which is to say, you cannot be compassionate.

So, let us begin this section on awareness by exploring how to cultivate it through mindfulness practice.

A Warning/Invitation

This chapter introduces you to the benefits of mindfulness for your health, wellness, and leadership journey. It also includes some general instructions on how to begin practicing it. Before I go into all that, I do need to tell you something—something that's both a warning and an invitation.

Mindfulness is much more than a tool for living and leading. It's a spiritual practice of letting go. Again, and again, and again. It's about releasing our unhealthy attachments—the things we think need to be ours, or need to be in place, for us to be happy.

When our cravings and fears rule us, we suffer. Things often do not turn out as we wish. Bad things happen, no matter how hard we try to ward them off. Good things fade or slip away, no matter how hard we try to keep them. Everything is always changing. Learning to loosen our grip, to be okay with it not being okay—this is the pathway to peace.

Letting go is hard. We're hardwired to hang on *so* tightly.

There's an ancient story of some monks sitting under a tree with the Buddha, eating lunch. Along comes a farmer in grave distress: "Venerable monks," he says. "Did you see my cows come by? I have a dozen cows, and they all ran away. On top of that, I have five acres of sesame plants, and this year the insects ate them all up. I think I'm going to kill myself. I can't go on living this way."

A powerful compassion fills the Buddha's heart, as he says, "No, my friend. We didn't see any cows come this way. I'm sorry."

After the farmer leaves, the Buddha turns to his students and says: "My friends. Do you understand why you are so deeply happy? It's because you have no cows to lose."

What are your cows? What are the things you think are essential for your happiness? Maybe it's money, or beauty, or reputation, or certainty, or achievement, or a certain person's love or approval. It sounds counter-intuitive, but, in the words of Thich Nhat Hahn, "The secret of happiness is being able to let go of your cows."[72]

71

Mindfulness will teach you to do this. When we build mindfulness practice into our lives, we begin to see our thoughts and emotions with openness and acceptance. We learn to stop struggling with ourselves and others so much. We stop overtrying and overdemanding. We begin to recognize when we're all caught up in our fears and desires. We start to trust that we really can let go. Then, the magic starts! We begin to relate to ourselves, others, our jobs, our families and friends, and our world *without* clinging and grasping, *without* pushing and pulling. A powerful and contagious *calm* starts to anchor us. It's then we know we're on the path to true wisdom and compassion.

The Science of Mindfulness

Imagine a miracle drug that was associated with the following in persons who took it regularly: decreased depression; decreased anxiety; increased ability to cope with traumatic circumstances; decreased substance misuse; increased overall cognitive functioning; increased ability to focus and concentrate; increased ability to cope with pain and stress; increased auto-immune functioning; decreased insomnia; increased overall happiness and well-being; increased satisfaction within the context of relationships; increased connection with others in the workplace. That's just the beginning.

You'd sign up for a daily dose of *that* right away, wouldn't you? The list I just rattled off constitutes a mere sampling of the health and wellness benefits linked to regular mindfulness practice. There are many, many more, and new studies are coming out all the time.

Practicing mindful awareness doesn't just change our experience of the world. It physically alters the squishy stuff inside our skulls. In a 2005 *f*MRI study, Sarah Lazar and colleagues discovered a correlation between the amount of time meditators spend meditating, and the thickness of key areas in the brain's prefrontal cortex (the brain tissue that lies just behind your eyebrow). What this means is that regular meditation builds and strengthens brain structures responsible for higher-order cognition, planning, emotion regulation, empathy, and impulse control. Since that seminal study, many more studies have linked mindfulness meditation with increased prefrontal gray matter, as well as blood flow.

You see, brain structure isn't fixed. It can be changed. This is usually referred to as "experience-dependent plasticity" (or just "neuroplasticity"). *You* have the power to *decide* to transform your brain, so that *you* become more attentive to others. More tempered. More insightful, rested, calm, pain-free, and decisive. Happier! And, of course, more compassionate. It's like the ancient symbol of the ouroboros, the snake eating its own tail. You use your will to change your brain, to strengthen your will. A mind bender! Literally!

Changing the Settings

Becoming more present isn't easy. It takes time, effort, consistency, and dedication. As Rick Hanson describes in his book *Buddha's Brain*, changing your brain and mind through mindfulness practice amounts to reconfiguring some deeply entrenched, evolutionarily primed, settings. It's about learning to "swim against ancient currents within your nervous system."[73]

First, we've evolved to view ourselves as separate from all else, and to take care of number one. Mindfulness, though, teaches us to experience the interconnection of things. We start to see that my happiness and your happiness are inextricably entwined. Mindfulness cultivates an interconnection mindset where we see that all of us rise (and fall) together.

Second, we've evolved to crave stability and sameness. Mindfulness, though, teaches us to dance with impermanence, to flow with the ever-changing nature of reality. Such deft mental and emotional agility is essential in a world that's changing ever more rapidly, and where organizations and teams often need to pivot quickly.

Third, we've evolved to be motivated by desires for good things and fears about bad things. Mindfulness, though, reveals to us that peace and contentment come when we remain unrattled by the pleasant and the unpleasant alike. We gain the ability to choose what's truly good in the long-term, versus what will give us the "Ooo!" (or keep us from the "Oww!") in the short-term.

Fourth, we've evolved to be constantly simulating reality— imagining what might happen next, and chewing our mental cud over what's already transpired. In other words, most of us are expert ruminators. Mindfulness teaches us to come back to here and now. We experience being aware, awake, and alive in *this* time and place, with *this* person or team. There is no other way to become truly vested in those we lead if we are physically present, but mentally (and/or emotionally) absent.

If you commit to a daily mindfulness practice of even ten minutes, you are literally growing wisdom in your physical nervous system. After a while, with patience and dedication, you'll start to feel it. It's the sense of being grounded. Open. Here. Seeing. Trusting. Bigger than your cravings. Larger than your fears. At home in yourself. Settled within the peace, strength, and love you already possess. Others will start to sense it, too. They will come to know that, in your presence, they are seen and safe.

Because it takes time and solitude, it's tempting to think regular mindfulness practice is selfish, but nothing could be further from the truth. Becoming an aware, present leader is the foundation of becoming a wise, compassionate leader.

Key Ingredients of Mindfulness Practice

At this point, perhaps you're saying to me: "Okay! I'm convinced! Mindfulness is amazing! But how do I actually *do* it?"

Mindfulness meditation practices generally have the following elements in common.

First, *a quiet environment*. Although you can become mindful anytime and anywhere, when you're first starting out, it's important to practice at a time and in a place where you are unlikely to be disturbed or interrupted.

Second, *a relaxed, yet alert, body.* Be seated, either in a chair or on a cushion on the floor, with your spine straight yet supple, your shoulders soft and dropped, your jaw relaxed, your hands resting quietly in your lap. You want to be comfortable, but not so much so that you fall asleep.

Third, *an intention to observe one thing.* Traditionally and most often, that thing is the breath. Become aware of the natural flow of the breath in and out of the body. Witness the cool inbreath as it fills your nose, windpipe, and lungs, and witness the outbreath as it leaves your body and disappears into space.

Fourth, *the re-direction of attention.* When thoughts, emotions, and sensations arise, take note of them. Observe them, but don't judge or worry. They are what they are. See if you can let them be there without becoming carried away by them. Then, gently shepherd your attention back to the feeling of the breath coming in and going out.

Fifth, *discipline.* Commit to practicing mindfulness meditation for ten minutes per day, for a week. The next week, perhaps extend it to fifteen minutes. The real gifts of mindfulness practice require regularity and commitment.

All of this sounds rather simple, but anyone who's tried it will tell you that it's not easy to stay focused on just one thing. The mind is a wild horse; a monkey in the treetops. It bucks and rears against stillness; it swings mischievously from thought to thought. I find that some days are easier than others when it comes to finding that sustained focus, but when I get there, it's truly lovely. Such a relief. In the spaciousness of mindfulness, I realize again that my thoughts and feelings are a *part* of me. However, as the *observer, I* am bigger than them. I can notice them, and then decide whether to entertain them. Then, once again, I can settle back into the clear and unclouded truth of my deepest being: simple awareness of the here and now.

More Ideas for Practicing Mindfulness

Meditative breath awareness is only one way to practice mindfulness. There are so many others! Here is a brief list of simple things you can try anytime.

- **Body scan.** Mentally scan your body up and down, searching for tense areas. Address them one by one, and gently invite them to relax. You might try saying, inwardly, "let go."

- **Belly watching.** Put your hand on your belly, lower your gaze there, take some deep breaths, and watch your hand go in and out as you breathe.

- **One cleansing breath.** Do a "big exhalation": Take in as much air as you can, hold, then exhale slowly while intentionally relaxing.

- **Heart-breathing.** Focus your attention on your heart. Call to mind good, soothing feelings, like gratitude, kindness, or love (perhaps by remembering a happy time with someone you love). Then imagine breathing that good feeling into your heart. Feel the goodness breeze its way into, and out of, your heart.

- **SIFT.** SIFT stands for sensations, images, feelings, and thoughts. Soften your gaze, take a deep breath, and then simply notice (1) two physical *Sensations*, (2) two *Images* your eyes can see, (3) two *Feelings* (or emotions) you are experiencing, and (4) two *Thoughts* currently in your mind.

Mitigating Unnecessary Hurt

This is a book about compassionate leadership—about becoming the sort of leader who helps mitigate unnecessary hurt and hardship.

No one denies that the Covid-19 era and all that's followed has brought added pain and struggle. As we saw in Part I, the compounded societal traumas of our time have deeply impacted today's workforce.

It's a basic truth of human life that we're all just trying to "make it" in the best way we know how. Life is hard. We suffer. In fact, Buddhism's first two Noble Truths are (1) everybody hurts, and (2) we hurt because we're constantly being whipped around by our unhealthy attachments (our fears and desires). These admissions are where the path of the Boddhisatva, the wise and loving warrior, begins.

If you're experiencing something especially painful—whether related to your leadership journey or not—I think you'll find that mindfulness practice can bring a good measure of relief from what's distressing you and causing you to suffer. It's about tapping into your own innate ability to free yourself from cycles that keep bringing you unhappiness—whether they be physical, mental, emotional, behavioral, or relational. It's *not* about finding the escape hatch. Unfortunately, there isn't one. If anything, mindfulness is going to ask you to dig deeper into, to stare more intently and lovingly at, the experience of pain. Something incredible happens when we stop running, numbing, and fighting, and open to the simple acceptance of what is the case right now. Peace, presence, and even joy can take root and begin to grow—even amid the hurt. This is what's behind the well-known quote, often attributed to the Dalai Lama: "Pain is inevitable, suffering is optional."

I want to close this chapter with a quote from Buddhist nun and teacher Pema Chödrön. Her words demonstrate to me the difficulty and hope of becoming more mindful, especially if you're in a moment where you're facing something challenging. May

Pema's words meet you exactly where you are right now. May they bring clarity, equilibrium, and strength to your heart and mind.

"Life is a good teacher and a good friend. Things are always in transition, if we could only realize it. Nothing ever sums itself up in the way that we like to dream about. The off-center, in-between state is an ideal situation… To stay with [the] shakiness—to stay with a broken heart, with a rumbling stomach, with the feeling of hopelessness and wanting to get revenge—that is the path of true awakening. Sticking with that uncertainty, getting the knack of relaxing in the midst of chaos, learning not to panic—this is the spiritual path. Getting the knack of catching ourselves, of gently and compassionately catching ourselves, is the path of the warrior."[74]

Discussion Questions

1. As you explored the concept of mindfulness and the practices mentioned in the text, were there any specific practices that stood out to you as particularly intriguing or appealing? Which mindfulness practices sparked your interest and made you eager to give them a try in your own life?

2. Reflecting on the various mindfulness practices discussed, which ones do you believe have the potential to enhance your awareness and deepen your sense of leadership presence? How do you envision incorporating these practices into your daily routine and how do you anticipate they will contribute to increasing your overall mindfulness and self-awareness as a leader?

CHAPTER 9
YOUR LEADERSHIP PRESENCE

I used to be an academic conference junkie. I've sat in countless Hilton ballrooms listening to lectures delivered by erudite talking heads, most of them unmemorable.

However, there's one I'll never forget.

A year or so into my first tenure-track job, I attended a panel discussion on Buddhist meditative practice and contemporary neuroscience. Normally such a panel wouldn't be anything too special; after all, the neuroscience of meditation is a popular research subject. In this case, however, several of the panelists were *themselves* Tibetan Buddhist monks. They were participating in a conversation with two other neuropsychologists on the mind- and brain-transforming effects of deepening one's awareness through meditative practice. For decades, these monks had spent most of their waking hours in meditation. It was a special honor to be able to listen to and learn from them.

I remember the moment when the monks walked into the packed ballroom. There was an almost immediate shift of energy. A weighty calm, a grounding gravity, a peaceful vitality set in. There were hundreds of people there, and every single one felt the change in atmosphere as the monks padded softly to their seats up front.

It was their presence. Something about it called forth a hushed, vibrant attentiveness in the mind and body of each attendee.

If you've ever been in the presence of a powerfully self-aware and other-attuned person, you understand the feeling I described. Certain people have a bearing or comportment that conveys calm, connection, and solidity.

My amazing friend Fern is one of these people. She meditates for an hour every morning, just as she has for years. When I'm with Fern, it's a bit like being with the monks on that panel. I sense her fixed attention, her genuine care, and her unshakable trustworthiness. I'm soothed, focused, and enlivened. When we walk together, my spine tingles with balanced well-being as we step along, listening and speaking in turn. I *feel* my feet on the earth. I *feel* the breath through my lungs. No matter what I am going through, no matter what I tell her, I *feel* known, welcomed, and deeply listened to. I always leave our meetings strengthened for whatever's ahead, no matter how hard.

Dual Awareness

The energy I've described, along with its effects, can seem a bit ethereal—even supernatural—but there's a scientifically explainable reason for its power.

The human brain uses the same neural systems to attune to *itself* that it uses to attune to *another person*. So if you're working on being an observant, caring presence to your own self (say, through regular mindfulness practice), this is, by default, going to expand your capacity to bring that kind of presence to another. Dual awareness is another term for this co-presence, which I like to envision as two sets of eyes—one looking inward, the other looking outward. Compassionate self-awareness becomes empathic other-awareness, and what's felt within one brain becomes a shared space of resonance between two brains.[75]

Dual awareness is the secret sauce of a wise and compassionate leadership presence. It can be described as the ability to maintain relaxed observance of your own sensations, emotions and thoughts, *while* paying sustained, non-distracted attention to another or others. Such a presence is palpable and powerful. It tends to elicit trust and concord with those around you. It's simply you being you, without pretense or fear. In Chris Johnson's words:

> When you can feel your own sensations while paying attention to another person, they can sense that you're fully with them without having abandoned yourself. Simply by

being present yourself, you provide the opening for others to engage more deeply as themselves too, because presence involves an ability to connect simultaneously with one's self and the thoughts and feelings of others.[76]

We're automatically drawn to such leaders. They're so fully *there*—so fully *themselves*—that we feel motivated and inspired just being around them. It comes from that sense of calm connection they so naturally and effortlessly radiate.

Such a presence cannot be faked or manufactured. It isn't something you can just *decide* to *do*—like adding a set of bicep curls to your morning workout. However, leadership presence *can* be developed and deepened. It's about practicing the skill of being more and more aware and connected. By practicing awareness and connection, we're "training to tolerate, expand, and cultivate capacity for ever more life to flow through us," as Chris Johnson says.

Deepening your leadership presence takes time, intentionality, and open-heartedness. It also takes understanding things that weaken awareness and connection, and therefore, diminish presence. Even when we try to be fully *there* (for ourselves, others, or both), we often find ourselves pulled away again by internal or external interferences. Let's explore three of the most common ones. I call them "presence-diminishing gremlins."

Presence-Diminishing Gremlin #1: Digital Distraction

You know how it goes. Someone's supposedly interacting with you. Then their phone buzzes or beeps. Suddenly their eyes surreptitiously dart down to their device. Meanwhile, they continue to nod and intermittently meet your gaze. Then their thumb starts to fly across the phone's surface. Maybe they even apologize to you. "I'm so sorry, I have to quick reply to this text!"

Does that make you feel uncared for? Dismissed? Invisible? Distrustful? Angry? Unmotivated?

If you said yes to those things, research shows you're not alone. Maybe the term "boss phubbing" is old hat to you, but

I only recently learned about it. Boss phubbing happens when you, as an employee, feel that your leader is distracted by their smartphone while in your presence.

A recent study of US adults working in various sectors found that when leaders are distracted by their phones, it undermines trust and decreases employee satisfaction—which, in turn, lowers job performance.[77] Another study showed that employees who perceive their boss as using a phone more often during interactions tend to feel socially excluded, which negatively impacts organization-based self-esteem.[78]

When we as leaders fall prey to the unrelenting pull of our smartphones, we chip away at trust and belonging in relationships. We undermine confidence and motivation in those we lead. Why? Because "phubbing" weakens and fragments our *thereness*. When our brains are halfway in our notifications and halfway in our here-and-now conversation, our energy and attention are uncontained and unpredictable—dotted across the landscape of thought and experience. We're "scattered," quite literally. Neither fully *with* ourselves nor others, we're caught in a kind of no man's land, between physical presence and psychological absence.

Others end up feeling semi-abandoned. Their experience is perhaps akin to what Dr. Pauline Boss calls "ambiguous loss," which is much more emotionally stressful than other types of absence or loss.[79]

If you're often digitally distracted and want to stop, here's what I recommend.

- Tell three people you trust that you're resolving to be less distracted by your phone. Invite them to ask you how it's going.

- Gradually increase the amount of time you physically leave your phone in your bag, desk drawer, or elsewhere (not on your person).

- Identify the five people who message you most frequently and let them know you won't be getting back to them as quickly (and why).

- Focus less on what you're not doing ("NO! *I am not* looking at my phone!"), and more on what you *are* doing ("YES! *I am* actively listening to this person or group!").

- When you're talking with someone and are tempted to check your phone, try "grounding down." This is where you imagine the whole lower half of your body becoming heavy, sturdy, and strong—magnetized down toward the earth. Like an ancient tree with massive roots, or like a crouched sumo wrestler—*whomp!!!*—you ground yourself down. Breathe. Be still. Feel gravity. Now, out of that sense of groundedness, refocus your attention on the person in front of you.

Presence-Diminishing Gremlin #2: Inner Conflict

For years, I've maintained a small psychotherapy practice. Most of my clients tell me they want to feel better in daily life. They want to be less anxious, less sad. They want to be more satisfied, more focused. They want happier, healthier relationships. In a word— they want that calm, fulfilled *presence* we've been discussing in this chapter.

Over time, I've discovered one hidden factor that often keeps people from it: chronic inward conflict.

It's normal to feel torn and unsure at times. This is especially true of leaders who are called upon to make important decisions with significant implications. While a patient, measured, collaborative approach is best, there is such a thing as getting caught in the mental mire of indecision. We simply can't decide what to do, which direction to go, what to say, how to be, to whom we should listen, or all the above. We're stuck.

When inner conflict takes root and doesn't resolve, it directly affects our mood and performance. We can become irritable, distracted, and apprehensive. There are physiological reasons for this.

Neurocognitive researchers have found that inner conflict, ambiguity, and uncertainty are largely processed in the anterior cingulate cortex (the same part of the brain that processes pain, both emotional and physical). Uncertainty is also associated with heightened noradrenaline release.[80] This means that when we remain stuck in confusion and unresolvedness about our direction, our brain processes it as *pain*—whether we're aware of it or not. Just like other forms of chronic pain, this distress becomes a weight that drags us down. It frequently shows up as anxiety—impacting our ability to control our thoughts, focus on tasks and people,[81] and be happy in general.[82] Such states make it nearly impossible to show up with mindful, compassionate awareness to and with ourselves and others.

Is there a big decision you need to make about your work, your relationships, your life? Have you been sitting on it too long?

In my work with clients, I often find that people know, deep down, what must be done. However, understandably, they're afraid of change, or worried about failing, or concerned about inevitable pain of repercussions. All of this makes sense. *And?* You deserve peace. You deserve inward integration. Such a strong, settled feeling only comes when you bravely face the conflict and work toward resolution, no matter the effects. It will strengthen your spine, soften your heart, and deepen your presence.

Presence-Diminishing Gremlin #3: Triggers

Flaming leaves against a gray October sky. Crisp apples off the orchard tree at our cabin on Lake Mille Lacs. The start of football. Hoodies. I used to adore fall.

Then last year, I found myself tense, preoccupied, and cranky during the whole month of September. The sudden cantankerousness was intense enough for others to point it out. What was going on?

Have you ever felt abruptly thrown for a loop, disoriented, or catapulted into defensiveness, worry, rage, self-recrimination, sadness, or some other negative state? Triggers are reactions that put us out of sorts. They can be initiated by internal (e.g., a memory) or external (e.g., a slamming door) stimuli. They can also be implicit (an unconscious association) or explicit (a conscious reaction). Whatever their source and structure, they immediately wrench us from the moment, wrecking our intentions to be mindfully present.

In my case, after reflecting on my autumn grumpiness, I realized I'd been a distracted, prickly person for several Septembers in a row. The trigger was internal and implicit. See, as I've aged, I've become less and less tolerant of cold Minnesota winters. The frigid darkness exacerbates my Reynaud's Syndrome, activates my Seasonal Affective Disorder, and aggravates my early onset osteoarthritis. Basically, as my body senses the coming winter, my whole being gets triggered. I'm bracing for an icy wave of months-long stiffness and pain. *Of course* I'm cranky and preoccupied!

Triggers are a part of being human. They are automatic self-protective reactions, and they are normal. Everyone has them. As leaders, we can either allow them to sabotage our presence, or deepen our awareness.

To investigate your triggers, try this exercise. Recall a recent moment when you were thrown off-kilter or seemed to lose hold of yourself. Now ask gently and nonjudgmentally: What physical reactions accompanied my response (e.g., bodily tenseness, flagging energy, nausea)? What behaviors ensued (e.g., highway speeding, staying in bed all day, slyly demeaning comments during a team meeting)? What emotions were involved (e.g., worry, irritability, self-righteousness)? What beliefs underlie my reaction (e.g., "I'll never be enough for her," "No one ever shows up for me," "I can't trust this," "I don't feel competent," "This should be different.").

Now, breathe, and try to soften, as you ask reflective questions. Here are some options to get you started.[83]

- Can I admit to blind spots and/or foibles in my leadership presence?

- What impact will it have if I admit to "not knowing"— e.g., not knowing what to do?

- Can vulnerability help or hurt me, my team, my colleagues/network, my organization?

- What can I do with the emotions that get stirred inside of me?

- Is my trigger due to a line being crossed? If so, how can I shore up my boundaries?

- Can I allow my emotions to be present while, at the same time, I decide to attend with care to the people, tasks, and things in my life?

If you want to become a more compassionate leader, it's crucial to take time to reflect upon (and, ideally, talk to a trusted other about) your triggers. It will solidify your (dual) awareness, strengthen your personal presence, and make others experience you as a trustworthy, grounded, and attentive leader.

Finding Center

Remember old fashioned radios? Remember the feeling of dialing into your favorite song on your favorite station? Finding center is a bit like that. You move past the static of your insecurities, distractions, annoyances, and anxieties. You tune into the strongest, wisest, clearest version of you. Chris L. Johnson puts it this way:

> "When mind, body, and spirit are aligned, personal power— the power to generate competent actions and to experience learning and satisfaction in living life—radiates from within. This state of unified alignment is called 'centering.'"[84]

Centering, or finding your center, is what fuels the attentive leadership presence we've explored in this chapter. It's also what fuels a happy and fulfilled human life. Centering begins with paying attention first to your *physical state*—your breath perhaps, or maybe the feeling of your feet resting flat on the floor. Our body, after all, is where all our feelings, moods, thoughts, and actions emerge. Then you bring awareness to your *emotions* in the moment. Is there overwhelm, joy, grief, gratitude, guilt, or something else? Next, you attend to your *thoughts*. Be curious. What recurrent patterns do you notice running through your consciousness? Simply observe, don't judge. Finally, having aligned the dimensions of your being, you can expand your awareness out to your environment, your relationships, your placement in time, and the larger mystery of life in which we are all enfolded.

When this deliberate self-inquiry is practiced regularly, centering can become a way of life. When, and as that happens, it cultivates incredible personal strength. It also instills the keen, expansive awareness that all compassionate leaders radiate. In the next chapter, we'll explore more practical ways to center and still ourselves in just this way.

Discussion Questions

1. Do you know a leader who embodies a sense of calm, connected, presence? When you are with this person, how does it make you feel?

2. How would you describe your relationship with distractions? Do you consider yourself a distracted individual? When it comes to your smart device, how self-aware are you of its impact on your ability to lead with awareness?

3. How do you experience triggers in life and leadership? What strategies can you implement to prevent these triggers from causing distress or setting you off?

CHAPTER 10
WHAT ARE YOU GOING THROUGH?

"Attention is the purest form of love," writes my favorite philosopher, Simone Weil. She believed the greatest gift we can give one another is our willingness to ask someone, "What are you going through?" and then simply to listen.

Recently I had the opportunity to work with a group of leaders in the financial sector. About six weeks after the compassionate leadership training program had ended, I heard from one of the regional directors, Jen. She wanted to thank me and share her story with me.

Jen told me that, in the past year, her mom had passed away unexpectedly, she'd discovered her husband was having an affair, her dad had been diagnosed with stage four lung cancer, and her dog had been hit and killed by a car. All in 12 months, all while raising twin kindergarteners and holding down a high-pressure job.

Now prior to the compassion training, *no one* at work had known about the stress and grief in Jen's life. During our follow-up call, she told me that because of the cultural changes that had come on the heels of the compassionate leadership journey, work was becoming a place where people wanted to know, "What are you going through?" As a result, Jen had risked being more authentic with several trusted colleagues. Then she began to receive some of the support she needed. As a human being amid a particularly grief-filled life moment, she simply felt *witnessed*, and it made a difference. In her terms: "The energy I'd spent stuffing my suffering while at work, can now be put towards my actual work."

Jen's words beautifully illustrate what a culture of compassionate awareness accomplishes: it *helps mitigate unnecessary struggle and suffering.* I say "unnecessary" because no one could make Jen's grief, trauma, and stress disappear. In this life, there are dark valleys through which we sometimes must simply walk. With the active building of a culture of compassionate awareness at work, however, Jen at least didn't have to suffer anymore with the painful and isolating pressure to pretend. Once that unnecessary hardship was removed, Jen found she could bring more of herself to her job, despite the ongoing pain in her personal life.

Tending to the Mystery of Others

Think of someone who's behaved badly around you lately. Maybe it was an ornery cashier at the grocery store. Maybe it was a driver who cut you off. Maybe it was your partner or colleague who said something that struck you as offhandedly callous, or even cruel.

What all went into their bad behavior? What led to it? Do you know? Are you aware?

You're probably aware of some of it—especially if you're close to them—but a crucial part of awareness is being aware of the *limits* of our awareness.

Every person, however bad their behavior, has been formed by a history of anguished and joyful moments that have brought them to the present time and place. This history is either totally or mostly opaque to us, and it is largely opaque to the person as well. I've come to believe there is something profoundly special, even sacred, about this opaqueness.

Simone Weil is famous for her writings on the unknowability of God, but she also talked a lot about the unknowability of other people:

> "Justice. To be continually ready to admit that another person is something other than what we read when they are there (or when we think about them)...perhaps something altogether different."[85]

We "read" others as best we can, but our interpretations are often woefully wrong. Weil believed justice requires constant awareness of the always partial, and sometimes totally mistaken, nature of our knowledge of other people.

What's required instead, according to Weil, is *attention*. By which she meant: a curious and open attitude wherein we wait to be surprised by the other person, and militantly curb our natural eagerness to prejudge. This kind of awareness immediately humanizes and dignifies the other person rather than confining them to the violence of a predetermined set of assumptions and expectations. For Weil, tending in this manner goes beyond mere ethics, and touches on spirituality. Why? Because humble, open-hearted, nonjudgmental attention to another person acknowledges them as a reflection of divine mystery—or what, as a Platonic philosopher, she often termed "the Good."

What can Weil's philosophy offer today's leaders? I believe there is an invitation here for a certain *quality* and depth of attention. It's more than asking engaging questions. It's more than putting down your phone. It's more than eye contact and head nods. All that helps, of course, but when we cultivate genuine reverence for the mystery and sacredness contained in the faces and stories of other people, we dignify them. We understand them anew. We open new avenues for their ongoing healing, growth, development, and wholeness.

People—especially people in pain—are hungry to be tended to and witnessed in this way. It is the only kind of attention that has the power to humanize, heal, and empower those entrusted to our guidance and care.

Aggressive Listening

What if you lead within an organization wherein attention, a la Simone Weil, isn't the norm? What can begin to build a culture of compassionate awareness?

In 1997, Captain D. Michael Abrashoff took over command of the USS Benfold. At that time it was one of the worst performing ships in the US Navy. "Everything seemed—desperately wrong," says Abrashoff in his book, *It's Your Ship*. "There was no energy anywhere—people were just showing up to collect a paycheck every two weeks. They were locking their passion and enthusiasm inside their cars in the parking lot and just bringing their bodies to work."[86]

Abrashoff's tack was to get aggressive—but not in the way you'd think. No one got a tongue lashing or a kick in the butt. Instead, every single one of the 310 crew members became the recipient of what he called "aggressive listening."

In his first six months as captain, Abrashoff sat down with each crew member for a 30-minute interview. His first priority was to connect with them personally (Where are you from? You partnered? Any kids? Why'd you join the navy? What are your hopes and plans for your future?). He learned a lot of them had tough backgrounds. Fully half had signed up because their families couldn't afford to send them to college, and a third had joined to get away from bad home situations—drugs, gangs, and other kinds of violence.

He writes:

> "Something happened in me as a result of those interviews.
> I came to respect my crew enormously. No longer were they
> nameless bodies at which I barked orders. I realized that
> they were just like me: They had hopes, dreams, loved ones,
> and they wanted to believe that what they were doing was
> important. And they wanted to be treated with respect."[87]

Abrashoff refused to reduce his crew to what he saw on the surface (disengaged workers). His open-hearted curiosity humanized them, forging connections that breathed new life into the entire workforce aboard the Benfold.

In the interviews, after he'd gotten to know them a bit, Abrashoff asked each crew member three questions:

1. What do you like most about the Benfold?
2. What do you like least about the Benfold?
3. What would you change if you were in charge?

Whenever someone gave a suggestion Abrashoff thought he could implement right away, he'd get on the ship's megaphone and announce the change. Something like this: "Everyone, Lieutenant Charlie says we should replace the ship's rusty bolts and fasteners with stainless steel ones so we don't have to sand and repaint them every year. Great idea, I'm ordering the new bolts today and we'll begin replacing them soon." (Abrashoff was famous for his liberal use of the ship's megaphone.)

The USS Benfold went on to become one of the navy's highest ranked ships.

If there are people in your organization who are checked out and running on fumes, try aggressive listening. Seek them out intentionally. Ask expansive questions. Listen with an open mind and heart. Expect to be surprised. Then, ask them what they'd change if they could. If they offer a good idea you can implement without much trouble—change it!—and let everyone know whose brainchild it was. This intentional, respect-filled tending from leaders communicates to folks: you are seen, you are valued, you are respected, and you belong.

More Awareness-Building Strategies

I want to close this chapter with three more practical, implementable strategies for leading with intentional attention and building a broader culture of compassionate awareness.

First, *ask purposeful questions.* The key to this is getting specific: Not, "How are ya?" but "Hey, I noticed you had some gnarly client interactions last week. How are you holding up?" It's important to check in and follow up on specific things. This communicates that you noticed what someone went through, you held them in your mind, and you cared enough to follow up.

Some situations call for more general check-ins. Find creative, purposeful ways to ask how people are doing. For example:

- What's something that's true of you today?
- What's taking up your headspace lately?
- What's getting your time and energy these days?
- What's something you feel confident or energized about right now?
- What's something you're unsure of, concerned about, or unmotivated to do right now?
- What's capturing your imagination lately?
- What can I do to support you?

Second, *try brave spaces.* These are regularly scheduled meetings where leaders ask open-ended questions and simply listen to those they lead. It's not about getting defensive. It's not about fixing. It's about leaders just witnessing what people are experiencing, with the intention of hearing them into speech (which is inherently compassionate and empowering). When done well, brave spaces can be powerful for culture change. This is especially true when there are challenges in areas of diversity, equity, inclusion, and belonging.

Brave spaces become especially effective when there are clear ground rules for safe and productive dialogue. Some examples of such ground rules include:

- Presume welcome and extend welcome.
- Refrain from fixing, saving, or setting straight others.
- When the dialogue gets tricky, turn to inquiry rather than advocacy.
- Speak for yourself, and not on behalf of anyone else. (This necessitates listening to yourself.)

Third, conquer your FOMO (*Fear of Missing Out*). Many of us fear that if we focus on and attend to the people we lead, we will miss something elsewhere, with dire consequences. This fear leads to an underlying state of being scattered and distracted.

The pace and complexity of modern life in a digital age compels us to simultaneously spread our attention in every direction. Many of us feel the need to be omnipresent, and we fret that if we aren't, something very bad indeed will happen.

Deepening our compassionate awareness means sacrificing our need to be all things at all times to all people. We need to let go of our fear that if we don't tend to something or someone right now, we'll miss out, disappoint, or drop the ball.

Here's what's true: You're *more* likely to miss out, disappoint people, and drop balls if you try to pay attention to it all. Computers are good at dual processing, but human brains are not. Deepening your presence and your awareness requires developing the faith and trust that all will be well "over there" while you remain "right here." Strive to courageously let go of the need to maintain constant control and oversight of everything (which is an impossible dream anyway).

Permission to Tend

There's an unspoken belief in business culture that people are first "getter-doners" and only secondly, human beings. As leaders of a wounded workforce in a VUCA[88] world, it's high time we switch that up in our heads. Compassionate awareness is adaptive; we were made for it! Everything about our evolutionarily shaped biological makeup tells us to tend with care to the people around us. It's more than okay to go with that inclination in the workplace—it's vital.

In the next section, we will explore how to deepen our tending through the power of empathy.

Discussion Questions

1. What strategies can you employ to incorporate the practice of active or aggressive listening into your workplace? How can you enhance your ability to truly understand and engage with others' perspectives and experiences?

2. From the list of questions provided in the "More Awareness-Building Strategies" section, were there any particular questions that stood out to you? Which ones resonated with you the most, and how do you think they can contribute to fostering greater self-awareness and connection with others?

Part IV
Empathy

CHAPTER 11
WIRED FOR RESONANCE

In the mid-1990's, an Italian research team, studying the premotor cortex of a monkey's brain, discovered something remarkable. Certain brain cells fired not only when the monkey ate a peanut, but *when the monkey observed another primate* eating a peanut.

These so-called "mirror neurons" were later discovered in human brains, leading scientists to conclude that we are built to create powerful representations (or simulations) of others' minds. In the words of interpersonal neurobiologist Louis Cozolino, mirror circuitry provides "a visceral-emotional experience of what the other is experiencing, allowing us to know others from the inside out."[89] We literally feel one another, in our very bodies.

Anatomically, mirror neurons lie at the intersection of prefrontal and parietal brain areas. This means they integrate visual, motor, emotional, and rational processing. In split seconds, we can seamlessly observe, feel, think, and act in concert with the states of others. Although it's an everyday experience and feels unexceptional, our profound ability to feel our way into others' experiences is at the very heart of what makes us human.

According to the "traditional" evolution narrative, our species developed via competition and extinction—"survival of the fittest," as Herbert Spencer first put it in 1864. However, it's also true that empathy and cooperation—the abilities to feel with, work with, and deeply understand others—have propelled human progress. In fact, our irreducibly relational brains have made possible the highest achievements in social/civic, ethical, technological, artistic, scientific, and other domains. Empathy empowers emergence.

The opposite is true as well. Absent dynamic, attuned interactions, people, like single neurons, wither and die. In neurons, this process is called apoptosis. In people, it is called isolation, grief, depression, anxiety, meaninglessness, and suicide.[90] Cardiologists have even found that loneliness is as bad for heart health as smoking or obesity.[91] As Gallup writers Rodd Wagner and Jim Harter put it:

> "We have evolved to care about each other. To be connected, and to feel like we are embedded in a community of support with whatever job we're occupied with. If we don't get that, if we feel alone, it automatically triggers our stress response system, telling us that something is wrong and we're in danger. In the rugged past, people who failed to work together didn't just have a bad day at work—they died."[92]

Empathy in Leadership

Given the close link between empathy and human thriving, it's no surprise that researchers have found empathic leadership to be crucial for organizational success—especially in today's high-stress contexts. Empathy fuels *retention*: According to the research group Businesssolver, 90% of employees say they're more likely to stay with a company that understands and empathizes with their needs. Empathy also lifts *morale* and fosters *belonging*. According to EY, 86% of employees believe empathetic leadership nurtures inclusion and inspires positive attitudes within the workplace.[93] *Innovation, and adaptability* are also powered by empathy. A 2016 multinational study by American and Malaysian researchers found that highly empathic managers are better able to observe and listen to others, thereby gaining new insights and perspectives on positive changes that can improve performance.[94]

Empathic leadership meets our existential need to be seen and understood. This need is most intense in childhood, but never really goes away. Empathy also meets our neurobiological need for emotional co-regulation. Humans rely on each other to balance, calm, and stabilize their minds in emotionally volatile times. When we feel connected, our threat detection system is soothed. The resulting sense of safety boosts our ability to show up as our best selves and do our best work.

Conversely, when empathy is lacking, employee dissatisfaction, disengagement, resentment, and resignation grow like cancer. As the workplace becomes more toxic and less human, performance and productivity wane, threatening the organization's health, stability, and long-term viability. This painful dynamic is at play in far too many organizations today. Businessolver[95] reports that, from 2022 to 2023:

- There was a 68% drop in HR leaders agreeing that "my organization is empathetic."

- There was a 68% drop in HR leaders agreeing that "my CEO is empathetic."

- There was a 78% drop in HR leaders agreeing that "my employees are empathetic."

All this begs the question: If we are *wired* for empathic interpersonal resonance, if it's so *good* for us as individuals and organizations, why is there such a dearth of empathic leadership in the workplace today?

Leaders Set Emotion Norms

Leaders set emotion norms in organizations. In big and small ways, they convey expectations about how much feelings matter, and whether certain feelings are more valid or valuable than others. People take their cue from leaders as they wonder things like: Is it okay to mention hard stuff here? Is it okay to talk about how current events are affecting my life? Is it okay to seek support when I'm going through a health scare, a divorce, a mental illness, or a problem with my kid, here? Or, at a very basic level: Is it okay to say I'm confused? Or stressed? Or, I made a mistake and feel awful? Or, I just solved a massive problem and think we should all put on our party pants for a hot minute?

These are questions having to do with trust and safety. They're questions about the extent to which people feel like they can be *fully human* at work, or whether they need to park anything that's feeling-related at the door, because it's too soft. Too squishy. Not productive. Not practical.

In most organizations, there are assumptions about what's valuable and not valuable in professional contexts. Feelings? Especially feelings of pain, confusion, overwhelm? Not valuable, not helpful, not clean, too irrational. Let's just get down to business. Leaders unwittingly promote this assumption all the time in organizational life—mostly in unseen and unnamed ways. Add to that the frequent over-emphasis on competition; the common fear of being seen as "weak," "soft," or burdensome; the increasing ideological polarization between people and groups; and the general lack of trust that's often present amongst workers. What you get is a very toxic brew. When these dynamics are left unchecked by leaders (or worse, furthered by them), it makes people feel dehumanized. That's when job satisfaction, performance, and loyalty start to really falter.

Leader Vulnerability

If leaders set emotion norms, this means that the extent to which *they themselves* are willing to express how they're really doing, tells others whether they too can be fully human at work. Leader vulnerability is an essential component of building a more empathic organizational culture.

Recent research by Adam Grant and his colleague Constantinos Coutifaris clearly shows that, when leaders risk being open and "fully human" with their team members, psychological safety and trust grow significantly.[96] In a field experiment, a group of managers was asked to share with their direct reports criticisms and suggestions they had received about their own performance.

Another group was asked to seek feedback from their direct reports about their performance.

One year later, the research team found that psychological safety improved when leaders shared their own developmental areas for improvement, but not when they sought feedback from their direct reports. In the latter case, defensiveness and inaction evaporated the connection that had been initiated by feedback-seeking. In contrast, "sharing feedback normalized and crystallized vulnerability as leaders made a public commitment to keep sharing and employees reciprocated."

Everyone understands how it feels to face your imperfections—to be told you need to do it differently or better. When managers and their direct reports were allowed to share in this experience together—to witness and "feel into" the vulnerable humanity of the other—accountability, trust, and psychological safety were instilled in an enduring way. Contrary to many leaders' fears, researchers found that vulnerability did *not* jeopardize managers' reputations as adept, effective, highly regarded leaders. Rather, it created the kind of trusting, resonant connection that bore higher engagement, greater innovation, and overall improved work quality.

Beyond sharing growth areas, what does leader vulnerability look like "on the ground"? Much of it comes down to a willingness to name your experiences, emotions, and uncertainties. This tells others that it's okay to feel things, to question things, and to risk sharing emotions and difficulties. The resulting psychological safety opens the way for powerful teamwork and problem solving.

For example, I have a good friend who, a number of years ago, held a high-ranking leadership position in a key division of the City of Minneapolis. In the days following the George Floyd murder, the division responded publicly to the incident in ways that ended up deeply hurting and offending some members of his team. Not long after, my friend, Teddy, found himself leading a virtual call in a large department meeting. He chose to begin that meeting by naming his own feelings in that moment:

"Everyone, this is not easy. My voice is shaking here, and I'm needing to take a few deep breaths, because I'm feeling a lot. Mostly, I'm feeling sad. I'm sad about the pain everywhere in our city, and here on our team. And I just want to say, before we go into problem-solving mode, that it's okay to be deeply sad, here. In fact, it's okay to feel a whole array of feelings. If we didn't feel them, we wouldn't be human. And more than anything, we here in this division need to hold onto our humanity."

Teddy went on to lead an incredibly productive and healing department meeting. He found that his decision to risk sharing his own emotions, and open space for others as well, helped facilitate greater understanding regarding the immediate team conflict. Beyond that, it laid the groundwork for beginning to repair long-held rifts and hurts around race, inclusion, and cultural difference amongst city division workers.

Redefining Professionalism

A few years ago, Dr. Sanja Licina, an executive at the research software company QuestionPro, asked a sample of workers from various industries about the kind of relationship they want with their manager. The survey revealed that upwards of 80% of workers agree or strongly agree that they'd like a closer personal and professional connection with their immediate supervisor.[97]

Without question, employees today want a genuine human bond with their leaders. This is especially true for younger generations. Millennial and Gen Z folks simply won't tolerate outdated workplace norms of cold aloofness upheld in the name of *professionalism*. To attract and retain promising, high-aptitude people, today's leaders must build a genuine empathic connection into the very fabric of effective management practice. It is eminently possible to embody "professionalism" while cultivating caring, authentic connections with others. In fact, I'd argue that in a world where 82% of employees say they would leave their position to work for a more empathetic organization, emotionally resonant professionalism is not only *possible*—it's *imperative*.

For many, the first step is to consciously give yourself permission to care, to connect, and to risk vulnerability. This can be easier said than done, especially in organizational cultures where the unspoken rule is to park all things personal, real, and feeling-related at the door, bringing only your task-fulfilling self to work. As many of today's work environments are still like this, it takes intentionality, strategy, and skill to integrate emotional intelligence and resonance into the fabric of what effective leadership and professionalism mean.

In the next chapter, we'll explore some practical, everyday ways to do just that.

Discussion Questions

1. Can you recall a personal experience with a leader who demonstrated empathy? How did they exemplify empathy in their actions and interactions?

2. When it comes to the emotional atmosphere you create, what kind of tone do you aim to set for others? How do your emotions and behaviors impact the people around you?

3. In the context of the workplace, how can vulnerability be embraced and expressed in a healthy manner? What actions and practices can foster a culture where individuals feel safe to be open, authentic, and vulnerable?

CHAPTER 12
THE ART OF EMPATHIC LISTENING

Ramona Sequeira took a breath, relaxed her shoulders, leaned forward and gazed intently into her computer's camera as she prepared to hear her colleagues' responses to the question she'd just posed. Even with the constraints of virtual communication, her presence projected a soothing calm and connection to her audience. Everyone on the call felt her willingness to listen and her genuine curiosity to understand their experience.

It was spring, 2021, and Sequeira was President of Takeda Pharmaceuticals U.S.A. and just beginning her tenure as the first woman to assume the role of Board Chair at PhRMA. (Later, she would become President of Takeda's newly created Global Portfolio Division.) She had set up regular virtual roundtable discussions with cross sections of the 3,000+ employees in her business unit.

The chief impetus for these roundtables was employee pain and confusion. Social upheavals from the previous year (including the Covid-19 pandemic and the murder of George Floyd and others) had deeply affected Takeda's workers. Many were seeking a response from leaders on issues like racialized hate and violence, and inclusion practices for minority employees. Other challenges loomed, too: confusion and concerns around vaccine mandates, the company's return-to-work policies and procedures, and more.

Empathic listening was the heart of Sequeira's strategic response. In the early days of the pandemic, she'd quickly recognized the need to flip the traditional leadership equation—80% business to 20% people—upside down. Over the years, she'd gained the confidence to define her own unique leadership style—one that aligned with her personal values and enabled her to become the skilled, courageously empathetic leader who was needed for this moment. A woman of color herself, she was aware of her biases and actively working to overcome them. She had learned the importance of sharing aspects of her story as a way of acknowledging what others were experiencing and feeling—including people very different from her. In this way, Sequeira was able to create spaces where employees could bring their honest questions, feelings, experiences, and stories forward—instead of the sanitized, buttoned-up versions.

During these roundtables, Sequeira was highly attuned to people. Her goal was not to opine about political stances, nor to defend company policies, nor to fix issues on the spot, nor to explain away challenges using corporate catch phrases. First and foremost, she simply wanted to recognize ways in which people felt confused and fractured. She wanted them to know that, amid their suffering, work was a place where they'd find a community of support, safety, trust, and advocacy.

Sequeira went into the roundtable meetings not with a rigid agenda, but with a handful of open questions about the topic at hand. For example: "What's on your mind regarding x topic?" "What are you going through?" "What are your roadblocks?" "What are you not seeing that you want to see?" "What do you need from me?" At times, the feedback she received wasn't rosy. Even so, she would remain calm and graceful, nodding her head thoughtfully and asking more open-ended questions. "Tell me more."

Sequeira was demonstrating the art of empathic listening. What effect did it have on the people and teams she led? Rushmie Nofzinger—former VP of Communications at Takeda and a frequent participant in these roundtables—says this:

I was blown away. It was the epitome of leadership. We had faith in her. We all knew that, wherever we landed with these issues, at least it would be done with the appropriate amount of care, concern, and thoughtfulness. Sequeira set a new standard and model for what leadership looks like.

Sequeira's roundtables didn't just give her employees a place to experience support in stressful times. It also made her a better leader. Because she took the time to understand the issues so deeply, she was able to synthesize the core challenges, and respond with targeted, effective solutions.

Ask Better Questions

One of the keys to Sequeira's success was her way of opening people up. During the roundtables, she knew how to use questions to set the stage for people to share authentically. Everyone knew they were safe, both psychologically and emotionally, and that their leader wanted to truly understand their concerns. So they shared. They felt seen and validated. Later, they watched as their raw feedback directly informed formal company responses to painful and stressful situations, as well as new benefit and wellness programs.

Asking better questions is crucial to mastering the powerful art of empathic listening. One easy commitment you can make right now is to drastically limit your use of the question, "How are you?" The research group QuestionPro recently surveyed 3,000 workers across various industries and companies, asking them how they respond when asked "How are you?" at work. A whopping 44% of people will always, or almost always, answer "I'm fine," rather than giving an authentic response. Only 3% will tell the other person how they're really feeling. If you really want to connect with your colleague (or team) and express genuine care and interest, look for better ways of checking in and initiating dialogues.

How do you actually do it? *How* do you ask better questions?

Following are four guidelines for posing queries that will set the stage for powerful and effective empathic connection with those you lead.

First, make your questions *purposeful.* The key to purposeful questions is specificity. You want your question to target something you know is pressing and relevant to the person or group. Sequeira, for example, had been working with the Asian American Employee Resource Group and knew they had some pain points she needed to better understand. In response, she posed the following question to her roundtable group: "Are we doing enough to foster inclusion and belonging with our Asian American colleagues?" Then she listened. The point here is to pause and ponder before a conversation or discussion, asking yourself how you can check in on some challenging issue this person or group has faced or is facing. Say it was an individual employee on your sales team who dealt with some rude customers last week. Instead of "Hey, how ya doing?" ask "Hey, I know you had some tough customer interactions last week. How are you feeling about those? Anything you need to process with me?" When you make your questions purposeful, you communicate that you noticed they experienced a challenge, that you're keeping them in mind, and that you care enough to follow up in a pointed and solution-focused way.

Second, make your questions *open-ended*. An open-ended question makes people feel respected and free. It's like you're inviting them into a sprawling field of wildflowers versus a narrow and confining tunnel. Let's say you're starting a one-on-one with a team member. Instead of asking whether their projects are progressing on schedule (a yes/no query that forces them into a clipped and closed response), try asking, "What's something you're feeling confident or energized about right now?" And/or "What's something you're feeling unsure of, concerned about, or unmotivated to do, right now?" These questions are likely to bring the status of the person's work projects to the surface, but in a way that honors autonomy, communicates respect, invites emotionally resonant connection, and initiates free-flowing dialogue.

Third, let *curiosity* permeate your questions. Nine times out of ten, we don't know what people are really going through, nor what's actually on their mind. An attitude of curiosity says, "I don't know what's true of you, but I'm eager to find out! Help me understand you! I'm listening!" This sets the stage for a vibrant, respect-filled conversation marked by mutual learning, insight, and innovation. Does it require you to set your ego aside? Become teachable? Correctable? Yes, to all of that! There are, however, few better ways to make someone you lead feel esteemed and valued than to be authentically curious about them. Don't fret that curiosity will make you seem weak or cause people to lose respect for you. To the contrary: because your curiosity helped deepen their own self-understanding and self-esteem, they will walk away feeling like your presence called forth what was best and most insightful in them. That, my friend, is the very definition of robust, impactful leadership.

Fourth, let your questions invite people to be *vulnerable*. There is no possibility of real, empathic connection without some degree of vulnerability. So, ask questions that encourage people's true humanity to come forth, and be willing to reciprocate in kind. Let's say you're leading your weekly team huddle and want to start with an "ice-breaker" that will build stronger and more empathic connections between you and your team members. Instead of asking, "What's your favorite flavor of ice cream?" try something like: "Is there something you've dreamed of doing for a long time? Why haven't you done it?" Or, "Fast-forward in your imagination. You're eighty-five, and you're looking back on your current self. What advice does your elderly self have for you today?" Questions like this welcome people into more humanizing and emotionally resonant spaces. They fast-track connection, belonging, and team synergy. Are they riskier? Do they get folks' heart rates up? Of course, but when you "go there" with those you lead, everyone feels that who they are, in all dimensions of their human being, matters. What a formidably tremendous gift.

Use Your Body

Empathic listening is the furthest thing from passive. It's a purposeful activity that involves use of your gaze, posture, movement, tone—your entire suite of bodily gestures, really. Nonverbals are the single most important element when it comes to communicating relational resonance with the people you lead.

Author Daniel Coyle[99] has spent years studying high-impact leaders. He's discovered that they all do certain things—mostly unconsciously. Here's Coyle's list:

- Profuse amounts of eye contact.
- Physical touch (fist bumps, handshakes, pats on the shoulder).
- Lots of short, energetic exchanges.
- Few interruptions.
- Lots of questions.
- Staying quiet, nodding the head, and leaning in while listening.
- Use of humor and laughter.
- Small courtesies (saying thank you, opening a door for someone).

Most of these impactful empathetic listening practices translate to virtual conversations. When you're in an online meeting, lean toward your computer's camera and gaze into it often. This creates the impression of direct eye contact. Take deep breaths while softening your shoulders, chest, and belly on the exhale. People feel your bodily energy even through their screens. Utilize attentive silence to coax people into speaking their truth to your attuned ears. Stay focused on the conversation—don't check texts, social media, or emails. Nod your head. Smile. Laugh. Relax your vocal cords and mirror the other person's tone of voice.

Such ways of using your energy, whether virtually or in person, both welcome others and convey personal power. These are the messages that get sent:

- I'm comfortable in my own skin.
- I'm unselfconsciously competent.
- I'm tuned into you.
- I hear what you're saying.
- I feel what you're experiencing.

- You're interesting.
- You're valuable.
- You belong.
- This is a connection you can trust.

When such subconscious messages are sent by leaders, the sky is the limit for their teams. There is no better relational environment for surfacing ability, cultivating innovation, heightening performance, and simply making people feel good about who they are and what they're contributing—especially when they are experiencing a measure of stress or struggle.

The Amygdala Effect

"Learning not to fear and learning to love are biologically interwoven." Surprisingly, that quote isn't from a spiritual guru or sacred text; it was written by interpersonal neurobiologist Louis Cozolino.[100]

When you feel anxious, stressed, or threatened, it critically thwarts your ability to engage in empathic listening. This is because the human fear response system is primitive, powerful, and fast. It's also very good at overtaking higher-order thoughts and emotions, like empathy and compassion.

The amygdala, the brain structure most directly responsible for fear responses, has had a large hand in shaping the survival and development of our species. Unlike other brain areas, the amygdala is fully operational even before birth. This means fear is, perhaps, the strongest early human emotion. In fractions of a second, our brains can appraise stimuli (inner experiences and outer events), initiating fight/flee/freeze/fawn responses long before conscious awareness. This amounts to a hijacking of prefrontal brain areas responsible for calm, connected tending to others. Here's when we suddenly find ourselves at our relational worst: we're unable to focus on what people are saying, both verbally and nonverbally. We might get fidgety, or simply draw a blank. We might find ourselves interrupting someone or getting irritated—maybe even explosive.

Perhaps we isolate from them in a cloud of "I can't even." Or, possibly, we find ourselves capitulating to whatever they say or suggest, unable to get a handle on our own authentic curiosities and questions.

These are just some of the interpersonal defenses of a human nervous system bathed in fear neuropeptides. I call it the amygdala effect.

The takeaway is this. If you want to become a generous, empathic presence to people in pain, finding ways to lower your own stress, fear, and anxiety is crucial. Neurobiologically, the way to do this is to strengthen the prefrontal structures and systems that are responsible for regulating your emotions. The amygdala is kept in check by its reciprocal relationship with the orbital medial prefrontal cortex (OMPFC). This brain area inhibits the amygdala's fear responses based on conscious awareness. How can you strengthen the OMPFC? With simple awareness-building and calm-inducing practices—many of which I've already mentioned in earlier discussions of self-compassion and awareness/mindfulness. For example: Just take a minute to slow down and take some deep, mindful breaths. Rhythmic sounds, sights, and movements. Nature. Self-compassion mantras (inner phrases/sayings). Consciously remind yourself of what's in your control, and what's just not. Anything, really, that gets your anxious mind away from the swirl of stress and worry and sinks it down into the feeling of your embodied present-moment experience, will help dampen the five-alarm fire raging within your amygdala and other lower brain structures. Your mind will then be freed to tend with empathy to the person or people before you.

Summing up: fear and care simply do not mingle. There are evolutionarily-shaped, neurobiological reasons for this. If you want to master the art of empathic listening, learn to live unafraid within your own mind and body. Feeling safe and secure within yourself is a non-negotiable prerequisite to becoming someone in whose presence others also feel safe, secure, and truly understood.

Now at this point, perhaps you are wondering where to draw the line with empathic listening in your leadership approach. After all, you are not your team members' therapist nor their best friend nor their spiritual advisor. You are their boss. Furthermore, taking on someone else's suffering can get overwhelming in a hot minute. You want to be present and supportive, but you must protect yourself from enmeshment in others' emotional negativity. How do you do that? How do you walk the line between caring connection and wise distance?

These are essential issues. We'll explore them more deeply in the next chapter about boundaries.

Discussion Questions

1. How can you enhance your question-asking skills? Are your questions purposeful, open-ended, and approached with genuine curiosity and vulnerability? In what ways can you improve the quality and effectiveness of your questioning?

2. Reflecting on the list of ways to use your body to foster empathic listening, which aspects stood out to you the most? How do you believe incorporating these practices can enhance your ability to listen empathetically and create deeper connections with others?

3. The importance of reducing fear, stress, and anxiety is emphasized as a crucial aspect of becoming a more empathic leader. Do you feel that any of these factors are hindering your ability to be an empathic presence in the lives of others? In what ways can you address and overcome these obstacles to cultivate a more empathetic approach?

Chapter 13
The Limits of Empathy

Empathy is a crucial element of compassionate leadership. On the other hand, empathy can also be a liability for leaders. Without three essential things—critical self-awareness, systems thinking, and boundaries—emotional resonance with others is likely to bring harm, not help.

Absent Critical Self-Awareness, Empathy Feeds Bias

When I was a Research Fellow in Princeton, Dr. Paul Bloom came to talk to our research team. His topic was, "Against Empathy: The Case for Rational Compassion" (also the title of one of his best-selling books).

Bloom argued that empathy gets in the way of our ability to make "rationally compassionate" decisions—choices informed by ethical, equity-driven principles.

Our social neurocircuitry has primed us to make emotional connections with people our brains perceive to be "ingroup" members—people close to us, people like us, and people apt to provide some benefit to us. There's nothing inherently bad about this situation. Our brains have been profoundly shaped by the tribal alliances that structured our social life in the deep evolutionary past. That's just the way it is.

Here's an everyday example. When I meet another middle-aged white mom who's trying to balance her professional career with parenting, I feel an immediate emotional connection. I get her feelings. I see her perspectives. I easily align with her stresses, struggles, and wins. I like her! I want to include her! I want to help her and encourage her! It's easy to be compassionate with this person!

What in the world could be wrong with that?

One word: bias.

Bias happens when I instinctively align myself with the experiences and interests of one person or group as opposed to another. Bias usually operates under the level of conscious awareness.

Returning to the example above, I wouldn't naturally feel the same empathic affinity for the struggles of a retired African American construction worker. In the latter case, powerful empathy is certainly possible, but not without two additional ingredients. First, I need *critical awareness* of sociocultural and emotional differences between us, whether real or perceived. Second, I need to make a *conscious decision* to intentionally *feel my way into* his situation, to the extent possible, through mindful awareness and empathic listening.

Let's take another example. Bobby is an HR Director in charge of hiring a crucial management position in his company. One day Bobby interviews a candidate with whom he immediately hits it off. This interviewee seems funny, smart, confident, and capable. Bobby can't explain it, but he just *likes* this guy from the moment he walks in. They went to the same university—wow! They had kids the same age—wow! They even went deer hunting in the same county each fall—wow, *wow, WOW!*

After the interview, Bobby prepares to tell the hiring committee that he's found their person, but he stops short because he realizes something. He's about to make a crucial personnel recommendation based purely on instinct-driven emotional resonance rather than self-aware rationality. As he critically questions his preference for the deer hunter, he realizes that the candidate he interviewed yesterday—a quiet Taiwanese woman with whom he found it hard to personally relate—is, hands down, better for the job. She's more qualified, more experienced, and has better references. He emails the hiring committee and says this: "I interviewed someone today with whom I'd love to go hunting, but who's not right for the job. Yesterday's candidate is our person."

Bobby's bias almost led to a huge hiring mistake. However, his critical self-awareness saved him and the company untold angst and expense.

Bias is a fact of life, but when it operates unconsciously, it leads to injustice, exclusion, and prejudice. In other words, attitudes and acts that benefit those like me, leave out or overtly harm those unlike me.

What's needed in today's world is people who are self-compassionately *aware* of their biased feelings, who *choose empathic listening* and connection amidst difference, and who *make rational decisions* that provide practical help to larger and more diverse groups of people.

Empathy is crucial. Empathy without critical self-awareness is calamitous.

Absent Systems Thinking, Empathy Feeds Chaos

Michaela is a manager whose weekly virtual team meetings have been taken over by Wendy. Wendy uses check-in time for lengthy, emotional expositions about her divorce process. Michaela feels for Wendy and wants work to be a supportive place, so she lets Wendy keep talking. Over time, she notices the meetings become less productive and efficient, with more frustration, disconnection, and disengagement.

Tom is a CEO who's facing the financial repercussions of five straight quarters of sharply dwindling sales. Six months ago, Tom's COO told him he needed to lay off 20% of his workforce to course correct. Tom brushed aside the recommendation because he couldn't stand the thought of upsetting the lives of so many of his workers. Now Tom is looking at a 50% or greater workforce layoff, and if things don't turn around quickly thereafter, bankruptcy.

When leaders empathize with the needs of the few, but ignore the needs of the many, bad things tend to happen. Problems fester, structures weaken, cohesion erodes. Chaos!

What's needed is systems thinking. This is a mindset that brings empathic awareness to different levels of a complex organization. Yes, you tend to individuals, but also to dyads, teams, divisions, consumers, the organization, stakeholders, the broader environment, and all the dynamic interactions between levels. Systems thinking guides you to identify the most pressing and pervasive needs, and make an ethical choice based on what will produce the greatest good and health for the greatest number of people and systems.

Does systems thinking rule out empathy? No. To the contrary, it expands it. It's about learning to attune to different layers of the system.

Before her meetings got toxic, Michaela needed to empathize with the system of her entire team, which was in a good deal of relational pain. Then she needed to do the "necessary evil" of speaking with Wendy and telling her that team meetings are an inappropriate place to do long-winded processing of one's personal pain.

Before his company was staring down Chapter 11, Tom needed to empathize with the system of his organization, which was in significant financial distress. Then he needed to do the "necessary evil" of laying off 20% of his workforce so the rest of the employees could keep their jobs, focus on sales troubleshooting, and get back to fiscal health.

Systems thinking leads you to see that actions benefiting the broader system (and more people) sometimes negatively impact smaller pockets of individuals. *That's okay.* As you'll see in coming chapters, you can practice radical acceptance of necessary evils, and execute the requisite actions, with great connection and care— in other words, with compassion. However, it's almost never compassionate to ignore larger systemic problems to protect the emotions of a smaller pocket of individuals. It only makes the situation more destructive and widespread in the long run.

Absent Boundaries, Empathy Feeds Burnout

No one has an endless capacity for empathic resonance with other people. Several neuroscientific studies on empathy in health care workers suggest that to be effective healers, doctors and nurses often suppress their empathic responsiveness to suffering patients.[101] It's not that they don't care. Rather, they hold the other person's pain at arm's length so that they can be more helpful to them.

When we know our limits and establish healthy boundaries, we become more effective, caring, and burnout-resistant leaders. Dr. Brené Brown's research has shown that people with clear boundaries are *more* compassionate, not less:

> "The clearer and more respected the boundaries, the higher the level of empathy and compassion for others. Fewer clear boundaries, less openness. It's hard to stay kind-hearted when you feel people are taking advantage of you or threatening you."[102]

What are some symptoms of burnout caused by empathy without boundaries? Here are some telltale markers:[103]

- You feel overwhelmed.
- You feel resentful toward people for asking for help.
- You avoid phone calls and interactions with people who might request something from you.
- You make comments about helping people and getting nothing in return.
- You feel irritable and "on edge."
- You're self-medicating in destructive ways (say, through food or alcohol).
- You have trouble focusing.
- You frequently daydream about dropping everything and disappearing.
- You have no time for yourself.

It's terrible to experience these burnout symptoms. Sadly, many who strive to be compassionate leaders feel them constantly. This is a tragic misunderstanding of what empathy and compassion mean and how they operate.

Hear this: It's never compassionate to allow the needs of others to engulf and erase your beautifully legitimate rights to time and space, to respect and freedom. Boundary-less empathy and self-sacrifice isn't honorable. It's irresponsible and self-destructive. Why? Because it teaches others to abuse and take advantage of you, and it robs you of the wisdom, love, and power you'd otherwise have to truly help.

Compassionate Limit-Setting

Compassionate leaders know when and how to say no. They make space and time to nourish themselves—physically, mentally, emotionally, relationally, and spiritually. They don't base their worth on pleasing other people. They refuse to believe the superhero myth that "I can do it all." They hold realistic expectations of themselves and others. They look for ways to experience appreciation for everything they do and bring. Without such practices, burnout is inevitable.

Empathic listening is essential, but you need to identify the point at which it becomes "too much" and starts to erode the strength and cohesion of you and/or others. Here are some signs that empathic emotional connections have turned into burnout-inducing emotional boundary violations:

- People are oversharing (too much too soon).
- People are excessively venting or dumping emotional information.
- People are spending inordinate amounts of time on emotional/personal connection, to the neglect of their work.
- People are invalidating others' feelings and/or telling others how they should feel.

- People are gossiping about the personal details of others' lives.

Limits protect people and make them feel safe. When you clearly and respectfully communicate what you're okay and not okay with, you model for others that they can and should do the same. For example:

- "I'm unable to process that at length with you right now, but let's set aside ten minutes in our next one-on-one to talk about it."

- "I hear that you've got a lot of heavy things weighing on you. I feel for you, but I don't feel equipped to help you. Have you considered talking with a therapist?"

When communicating boundaries, the key is to balance connection with assertiveness. Strive to be clear, kind, and direct with your words.

Will everyone like your boundaries? No. In fact, you're likely to get push-back from other people. Additionally, if overextending yourself on others' behalf has become habitual for you, a part of you will feel guilty when you begin practicing boundaries. Many of us have spent our whole lives feeling guilty for having wants and needs. So, when remorse fear, sadness, or awkwardness arise, remind yourself that it's profoundly healthy and compassionate to set boundaries. Others have boundaries you respect, and you deserve them, too. Until you stop basing your self-worth and confidence on whether others like you or are happy with you, you will never be free.

What about when someone is sharing something painful, stressful, or challenging, and you want to show empathy, but you're feeling a bit overwhelmed? Here's where *internal boundaries* become crucial. It's possible to tend effectively to someone in pain – to listen well, to offer supportive words and presence – while at the same time creating some healthy inward distance from their pain.

You can say to yourself:

- "Suffering and stress is terrible, and it's a normal part of life."
- "This person's story is not my story."
- "I can bring relief, not resolution."
- "I'm a supporter, not a savior."

Phrases like this, said internally, help keep compassionate connection while maintaining a measure of protective emotional distance.

Summing up: wise, effective empathy looks like balancing profound emotional resonance (on one hand) with a sharpened awareness, expanded perspective, and a firmed-up commitment to boundaries (on the other hand). Because each situation is different, there's no blanket approach to embodying wise and effective empathy. However, the more you practice this balancing act in new situations, the more you learn to trust that you can lead in a way that's as intelligently strong as it is caringly connected—which is the very definition of compassionate leadership. For most leaders, this is the work of a lifetime. Let's turn to explore some strategic actions and approaches that can help guide you in that vital endeavor.

Discussion Questions

1. When faced with the statement "Bias is a fact of life," and the idea of focusing on awareness rather than trying to eliminate biases, what were your initial thoughts? In what ways do you believe you can further develop in this area of self-awareness and understanding your biases?

2. Did you find yourself able to relate to the examples of team meetings lacking structure? Considering the potential of systems thinking to revolutionize team dynamics, how do you envision implementing this type of focus within your own team? What steps can you take to embrace a more systematic approach and enhance collaboration?

3. Establishing healthy boundaries is presented as one of the most challenging tasks in this book. Did any of the "telltale markers" resonate with you, indicating signs of burnout resulting from a lack of boundaries? How do you think you can address and establish healthier boundaries in your personal and professional life, and what benefits do you anticipate from doing so?

Part V
Action

CHAPTER 14
PRACTICAL STRATEGIES FOR
COMPASSIONATE ACTION

"People do their best work for people they love and are loved by."
— Paul Batz

First century philosopher Philo of Alexandria, is famous for his wise saying: "Be kind, for everyone you meet is fighting a hard battle." If current mental health data is any indication, the battles are especially intense these days. The National Institutes of Health reports that one in five Americans is struggling with a mental illness, with anxiety topping the list of ailments.[104] More telling evidence comes from ResumeLab,[105] which surveyed 1,000 employees in 2023 regarding mental health. They found that 68% have taken time off work due to mental illness, and 58% feel mentally or emotionally unsafe in the workplace.

Common strategies to fight emotional suffering at work include encouraging employees to meditate, exercise, and take breaks. These strategies are helpful, but they're not enough. Neurobiologically speaking, when people are emotionally dysregulated, the single most effective intervention is safe, trusting, and emotionally resonant relationships with other humans. We are built to help one another stay calm, grounded, and content. This shared energy of well-being is sometimes called "emotional co-regulation," and it's a key outcome of compassionate action in any human community (including the workplace).

In these last three chapters, you'll get lots of practical strategies for active care as well as accountability-building challenges so you can begin to build a more compassionate workplace culture. Care and candor are equally important when it comes to leading in a way that mitigates peoples' stress and pain while fueling their motivation to succeed.

Before we dive into strategies, be assured that the awareness and empathy-building practices we've already discussed are, *in themselves*, highly effective acts of compassionate leadership. As renowned compassion researcher Jane Dutton says, "Compassion is action in the face of not-knowing." Often, someone else's distress leaves us feeling helpless—we just don't know what to do. Dutton and her research team have found, however, that some of the most effective compassionate action in the workplace comes from people who have absolutely no idea how to convey support in the face of pain, but who decide, nevertheless, to do *something*. Many times, that "something" is a simple heartfelt check-in (awareness) and/or the gift of a listening ear (empathy). As one of Dutton's study participants said: "If you don't know what to say, say anything."[106] Remember that your simple presence, attention, and willingness to feel your way into the other person's perspective are themselves powerful interventions.

Beyond intentional awareness and empathy, other strategies abound. Let's consider a handful of them. What follows are seven action points that will help alleviate distress in the workplace by building stronger and more supportive connections between the humans therein.

Slow Down

In their book on compassionate leadership, Hougaard and Carter title one of the chapters, "Busyness Kills the Heart."[107] This phrase gets to me every time I hear it. In my own life, it's often true that busyness crowds out what's best in me—namely, my abilities to tend to, care for, and connect meaningfully with others. Probably, like you, I'm much too busy most of the time. I don't want my heart (or others'!) to shrivel because of my packed schedule. To be honest, that threat is often very real.

Case in point. Recently I missed seeing a goal my son made during a soccer game because I was looking down. What was I looking at, you ask? A Microsoft Word document titled "The Compassion Advantage," on my laptop. Against my better judgment, I'd brought my computer to Bennett's game because I was intent on finishing a section *in this very chapter* on compassionate action. I had justified bringing my computer to the game by telling myself, "I'll just putter with the document here and there while Bennett's not on the field." It was the wrong call. I'll never forget the way my heart sank when, after the game, Bennett came up to me with hurt and anger in his sweet face and voice. "*Mom.* You were looking at your *computer* when I scored! You totally missed it. You hurt my feelings so much!" The irony of withholding my compassionate attention to my own son so that I could make progress on a book on compassion wasn't lost on me. It was one of the lowest points in my ongoing quest to be an excellent (and compassionate!) mom *and* professional.

I share that story to assure you that *I get it.* I get how hard it is sometimes to slow down and pay uninterrupted attention, especially when we are all so pressed for time, with too much to do. However, it remains the case that the greatest gift you can give those you lead (or parent!) is your attention, and attention takes time and courage. You must find the inward resolve to slow down, let other things lie, and clear out uninterrupted minutes to be fully present. If you're a manager, there's no substitute for consistent, focused, one-on-one meetings with direct reports. This is especially true when there's added pressure, noticeable disengagement, suspected confusion, or general underperformance.

When you spend your energy and minutes being present to people who are struggling, it can seem like the exact opposite of productive. After all, your own to-do list doesn't lighten just because you're prioritizing people over tasks. This is why it's courageous. Rest assured, though: taking time to slow down, ignore your inbox, sideline your projects, and devote your time and attentional energy to people are some of the most valuable things you can do. This is true in *all* spheres of life (including kids' soccer games!).

133

Use Feeling Words

Words make worlds. Emotions are a huge part of everyone's everyday experience, yet many leaders refuse to use emotion-laden terminology in the workplace because they insist on "keeping it professional." Here's what Kim Scott says about that particular injunction:

> *"That phrase denies something essential. We are all human beings, with human feelings, and, even at work, we need to be seen as such. When that doesn't happen, when we feel we must repress who we really are to earn a living, we become alienated. That makes us hate going to work."*[108]

If you want to build a culture that's humanizing and healing, you must normalize emotions. Part of that means using emotion-friendly language in everyday workspaces like team meetings, emails, and one-on-ones with direct reports. Right now, ask yourself: How often do words like "love," "compassion," "hope," "care," "grief," "advocacy," "solidarity," and "empathy" enter your communications? It's a question worth asking. If the answer is "never," "seldom," or "sometimes," I encourage you to experiment with more feeling-laden language in your communications. It's a simple shift, but it can make a big difference because it gives implicit permission for people to bring their whole selves to work.

Call out Kindness

Compassionate action in the workplace often has a grassroots quality. Someone notices suffering, feels empathy, springs to action, and others follow. These things should be noticed and praised by leaders in the organization.

A friend of mine was at the breaking point trying to care for her ailing father, parent her middle-school-aged kids, and manage her high-pressure job. A work colleague noticed my friend's stress and created a campaign to get people to volunteer to drive her kids to sports practices, and even take her father to some of his medical appointments. This act of care made a massive difference in my friend's life. It was what got her through one of the most stressful seasons she's ever lived through. The carpool campaign did something else, too: it earned my friend's colleague a surprise "Kindness Award" (with a significant monetary bonus), which was given to her publicly by the company's upper management.

Compassionate action in the workplace deserves intentional and consistent recognition. In addition to kindness awards, one idea would be to start a quarterly (internal) "Compassion Hero" e-newsletter wherein you do a short, glowing write-up about one employee's act of kindness toward a colleague, client, or customer.

When people know their caring efforts are being noticed and recognized, they are more likely to continue those efforts. Over time, this can result in noticeable shifts within the organization's culture.

Believe (and Expect) the Best

Our beliefs about people create people.

In 1968, Harvard psychologist, Robert Rosenthal, published his now famous study on the so-called Pygmalion Effect. First and second grade teachers were told at the beginning of the school year that three specific students in the class were intellectually gifted, but not to treat them any differently than the others. The truth was that those three students hadn't shown evidence of being more gifted than any of the other students. At the end of the academic school year, those three specific students had significantly higher intellectual performance scores than others in the class. The teachers' mere *expectation* of the students' abilities helped usher them into the excellence that was waiting for them all along.

That's how powerful your beliefs about other people are.

Let's consider a real-life example of the Pygmalion Effect at work. Nicole Pullen is Head of Safety and Compliance ANZ at Fujitsu General Australia. Recently, Pullen told me how her senior leader, COO Clinton Goodwin, helped unlock her potential by raising expectations regarding her own leadership skills and style. After noticing that Pullen had frequently been overlooked for promotions throughout her sixteen-year tenure at Fujitsu, Goodwin began mentoring Nicole in areas related to boundaries, resilience, interdependence, self-compassion, and direct communication. He showed her how to ditch her "pleaser mindset," stop asking approval-seeking "micro-questions," and unleash her hidden gifts as a strong guide to (and mentor of) the people she led. Whereas Pullen used to struggle with fear of being judged, ignored, or belittled, she is now a bold, caring, connected, and highly effective manager at Fujitsu. Goodwin's bar-raising high expectations, along with attentive mentorship, helped Pullen grow into the greatness that was there all along.

Think of someone who's struggling or not living into their potential. Simply by believing the best in them, holding high expectations for them, and investing time in cultivating the greatness you see in their future, you can empower them in incredibly positive ways. That's what compassion in action does. It creates, renews, heals, and emboldens.

Say "Yes" to Flex

What is your kneejerk reaction to someone asking for more flexibility regarding their work location, hours, and/or scheduling? Do you immediately think: "No, it's too chaotic. I don't have the bandwidth to re-think all that. I can come up with a way to let them down gently and insist on the status quo." Or is there curiosity, openness, and generosity regarding how you might work with them to meet the demands of their job while maintaining more harmony and ease in their personal life?

Mandy was an HR Director who was helping one of her managers, Shawn, handle a situation with Shawn's team member who was struggling with depression. Chelsea, the remote-working team member, had recently asked Shawn if she could cut down on her work hours due to challenges stemming from her mood disorder. Less and less was getting done, largely because Chelsea required frequent morning rests/naps (thus missing morning meetings and blocks of work time), and now she was asking for more time off. Chelsea's coworkers were frustrated because they'd had to pick up her slack, and Shawn initially loathed to give an inch. He feared lowered productivity and heightened team conflict.

Mandy urged Shawn to avoid dismissing Chelsea's request outright, to ask questions, and to work toward a creative solution. Shawn did just that. As he listened to Chelsea, he discovered several things. First: Chelsea's depression was worse in the mornings, but afternoons and evenings felt much better in terms of mood and energy levels. Second: Chelsea wasn't taking advantage of the company's EAP Counseling Program, which was included in her benefits.

A strategic solution emerged from several listening sessions. Chelsea began to utilize her morning hours for rest, light exercise, and weekly EAP-facilitated counseling sessions, while the bulk of her working hours shifted to afternoons and evenings. Shawn needed to reschedule some regular team meetings, but this turned out to be a small price to pay. Within a few weeks, Chelsea was feeling better, and was able to take back some of the projects she'd passed to other team members.

If Shawn had dismissed Chelsea's original request outright, Chelsea's work performance and mental health would have likely continued to deteriorate. This would have further strained the team, and likely would have cost Chelsea her job. The "yes to flex" mentality, that Mandy helped Shawn lean into, afforded Chelsea emotional support and an opportunity to shine again at work. It also alleviated resentments and workload inequalities in the larger team.

If someone on your team is asking for more flexibility, ask questions and find out how creatively accommodating you can be. If you are nervous about a change in someone's schedule or work location backfiring, see if you can say "yes" to an initial trial period. Formulate clear expectations for performance during the period, and set a date when there will be a reassessment. When you say yes, it's essential to do so with clear provisions and expectations for performance.

Make a "To-Be" List

If you lead a team, one of the most compassionate things you can do is provide experiences in which people can connect with themselves and others at a deeper, more human, level. Conversations around meaning, purpose, and value can open chances for folks to be vulnerable and talk about who they are becoming—not just what they are accomplishing.

All work teams have to-do lists, but what about switching it up and trying a "to-be" list? Ask everyone to ponder: What are the ways you want to be in the world—the character attributes you most want to embody? Generous? Focused? Unafraid? Self-aware? Creative? One way to ask this is to have folks envision themselves at age 90, sitting on a park bench, reflecting on their life. What do they want to be able to say about the way they lived, loved, worked, parented, etc.? Have everyone (including yourself!) list five traits they'd like to focus on cultivating in themselves in the next six months. Ask them to share those traits with one another. Then open the conversation further, inviting everyone to create a "to-be" list for the team by focusing on common attributes that individuals named. In future meetings, you can use the team "to-be" list to reconnect at a personal level by talking about shared meaning, purpose, and character development.

See Invitations for Change Within Stories of Pain

When you create safe spaces for employees to speak openly about their struggles, sometimes you're going to hear less-than-rosy stories. When you do, it's easy to feel nervous, defensive, and frustrated. After all, you want those you lead to be happy!

Here's the thing though. Those very stories of pain and confusion often hold clues for new and positive changes that can or should be made within the team or organization. This is why you should actively work to view stories of pain as gifts. Thank people for their courageous vulnerability in sharing, and interpret their story as a live invitation for positive betterment rather than a dead-on-arrival decree of inherent badness.

In one of her Black Leadership Council roundtable conversations, Takeda executive, Ramona Sequeira (mentioned in Chapter 12), heard a painful report from Jory, one of her team leads. Jory overheard a sales coworker making disparaging "joking" comments about the majority black city neighborhood in which Jory had grown up and currently lived. "That place is a total concrete desert; I get depressed every time I have to go near it," his colleague had offhandedly said on a recent call.

In the roundtable, Sequeira listened to Jory's justifiable upset about the insensitive, racially charged insult to his home neighborhood and the people therein. "This neighborhood is my home—it's where I live, and where the people I love most live," said Jory. "And people think it's funny."

Ramona empathized with Jory's dismay, confirmed that such comments weren't okay and why, and then asked everyone a strategic question:

> "What is Takeda doing to boost quality healthcare availability in this neighborhood? How do we make sure patients have the right diagnoses, doctors have the right information to provide the correct diagnoses, and every person who needs it has access to the medicines they need to live their best life possible?"

Sequeira's query kicked off a months-long initiative to make Takeda's life-transforming medicines more available and affordable to the people living in Jory's hometown. In listening to Jory's very personal and painful story, Sequeira saw an opportunity, not just to speak against prejudice in the workplace. She also recognized a powerful opportunity to improve the health and well-being of the people living in of one of her esteemed colleague's home communities.

More than an actionable response to race-based cultural insensitivity in her organization, Sequeira's approach was a way to dig deep into an individual employee's struggle, finding therein opportunities for both business growth and community-directed compassion to support greater health equity.

Perhaps by now you're thinking, okay, when are we going to talk about the tough stuff? When are we going to talk about how to make difficult decisions, hold people accountable, navigate conflict, and provide corrective feedback? These things are essential to leadership—all leaders must do hard things. In the next few chapters, we'll explore how to do them with heart.

Discussion Questions

1. Among the seven action points presented in this chapter to alleviate workplace distress, which step resonated with you the most? Additionally, which one of these action steps do you already find yourself practicing or incorporating in your work life? Be encouraged by what you are already doing!

2. Considering the seven action points provided, create your own personalized action plan for gradually implementing these steps within your workplace environment. How do you envision introducing and integrating these points into your work culture? What specific strategies or approaches will you employ to ensure their effective implementation and positive impact?

CHAPTER 15
HARD THINGS WITH HEART:
COMPASSIONATE ACCOUNTABILITY

My friend Kate is the CFO of a company that makes snack foods for kids. A while back, a member of her team screwed up royally.

When you're making kiddo snacks, there are certain chemical ingredients you need to make sure *aren't* in the manufacturing recipes, because they're a health hazard and they're illegal. One of Kate's employees, Dave, put in a massive order for some snacks to be made at their overseas manufacturing facility, but failed to notice that a toxic and illegal ingredient was included in the recipe.

The snacks got made, and when they arrived at the US shore, you can guess what happened. The authorities tested them, the bad ingredient was discovered, and the whole lot had to be confiscated and discarded.

It was a $2M mistake.

I'll let you know how Kate responded to Dave a bit later in the chapter. For now, I want you to imagine you're Kate. Yesterday, you discovered this huge, expensive oversight. Today you're about to meet with Dave to discuss the situation. Dave walks into your office (or enters the virtual call).

Question: *Which non-optimal leadership response would tempt you most?* Simply make a mental note of your answer—it will help personalize the rest of what follows.

- **Mean Boss:** Augment Dave's mistake, yell at him, and perhaps even fire him on the spot so he understands how terribly unacceptable this is.

- **Avoidant Boss:** Ignore Dave's mistake and decide, last minute, to make the meeting about something else so you can deal with it later.

- **Over-Empathizer Boss:** Minimize Dave's mistake and console him; he's likely to feel awful anyway, and you don't want to make it worse for him.

What Makes Hard Things Hard?

Research shows that when leaders must carry a "necessary evil," like informing someone of a layoff or underperformance, they often feel anxiety, shame, and anger.[109] Why?

Science makes it simple. We're all social animals with social brains. When there's social tension—a situation that in some way threatens social harmony and stability—our threat detection systems kick in. This is because, in our species' ancient hunter-gatherer past, social harmony and stability meant safety, while social tension and instability meant danger. Deep down, our brains know instinctively that individual thriving is dependent on social concord.

For example, when we need to have a corrective conversation with a colleague; reinforce accountability on a project timeline; eliminate someone's position; or make a decision that we know colleagues will find unpopular, the primitive parts of our brain get fired up. We sense *threat*.

That tempts us toward the three non-optimal responses I mentioned earlier:

- Fight (mean boss)
- Flee/freeze (avoidant boss)
- Fawn (over-empathizer boss)

What can we do to avoid these non-optimal temptations as leaders—*all* of which are rooted in our brain's fear neurocircuitry?

Compassionate Accountability

Effective leaders consciously work toward something I call "compassionate accountability."

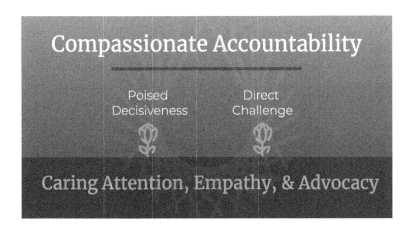

In this approach, the "accountability" elements of poised decisiveness and direct challenge are natural outgrowths of a robustly compassionate leadership style. The soil or substrate is caring attention, empathy, and advocacy. Contrary to Kim Scott,[110] I don't think it's a matter of *balancing* care and candor, rather, I think candor is one of the *outworkings* of personal care done right.

In this chapter, I'll introduce you to two essential ingredients for fostering Compassionate Accountability in your self-understanding as a leader, and in the culture you help to shape in your team and organization. The ingredients are:

1. Clarifying expectations
2. Receiving and relaying feedback

My confident hope is that, after reading this chapter, you'll be empowered with knowledge, inspiration, and the tools to do "hard things with heart"—to lead in a way that emanates wise care and engenders genuine trust.

Clarifying Expectations

Anytime you feel frustrated, overwhelmed, scattered, and anxious (I call this FOSA), it's often a sign that more clarity is needed. This is true in a lot of domains, not just work. Clarity is a prerequisite for accountability.

Not long ago it dawned on my husband and me that we needed a lot more clarity in our house when it came to our six-year-old son's behavior. What clued us in? We realized we often felt frustrated by him, disappointed in him, and annoyed with him. However, we were so busy that we hadn't taken the time to sit down and ask ourselves why. What, specifically, was not working about what he was doing/not doing?

We pushed ourselves to get clear on what *exactly* was annoying us and why. Examples: Every single time we'd try to talk to one another, he'd interrupt us, which was hurting our connection. Every night at dinner, he'd fidget and find excuses to get up from the table, which was disrupting our meal and conversation. Every time we said he'd had enough Pokémon Go, he'd whine for ten minutes, begging for more time to play.

Once we got clear on what *wasn't* working, we knew what we had to do.

We sat down for about 90 minutes and wrote "Hollingsworth House Rules." This includes a list of expected behaviors (e.g., making the bed, taking out the garbage), and behaviors that aren't allowed (e.g., interrupting, whining, stalling). It includes clear consequences for doing not-allowed behaviors and clear rewards for doing expected behaviors. The three of us had a family meeting (which involved some hot chocolate and marshmallows) and explained the expectations. Bennett was truly happy to know what was up in terms of expected behavior, consequences, and rewards. Our household has been so much more peaceful since then.

Obviously, discussing expectations in a professional setting looks different than discussing a simple rules list over a mug of hot chocolate. But the point remains true: Clarity is a prerequisite for accountability.

Getting Clear Yourself

Research shows there are a lot of workers out there who feel murky about their role. Gallup recently found that less than 40% of young remote workers clearly know what's expected of them on the job.[111] Does that hint that there are a lot of Gen Z workers sitting at home not really doing their job because they haven't put forth the effort to understand what, how, and on what timeline they're supposed to be getting stuff done?

Well, yes.

It also points to a lot of bosses out there who aren't communicating expectations clearly and consistently, especially with remote team members. It's likely because they haven't taken time to sit down and ask themselves what is and isn't working, what priorities need to be put in place, what changes need to be made (processing with their manager, too), and how best to communicate expectations to each person on the team.

Only after *you yourself* are clear on priorities, expectations, problems, and possible solutions, will you be able to communicate that to others.

The problem is, as a busy leader, you're often so focused on putting out your own fires that you haven't taken time to just look at the situation and ask, "What's the situation on the ground, how does it look from different angles, what might our options be, and how can we get crystal clear on the way forward, as a team?"

To create clarity within your own mind, ask yourself this question: Where do I feel FOSA (frustration, overwhelm, scatteredness, and anxiety)? Then follow up with these questions:

- *Is the FOSA there because I/we are focused on tasks, activities, or projects that fall outside our core mission as a business or team?*

- *Is the FOSA there because I/we are doing "good" things that are keeping us from the "best" things?*

- *What are the positive outcomes (rewards) for accomplishing the "best" things? What are the negative outcomes (consequences) for not doing so?*

Your answers will give you clues to areas where clarity is needed.

Clear is Kind: Communicating Expectations

My friend and colleague David Horsager says: "People trust the clear and distrust the ambiguous. Confusion breeds fear, frustration, and lack of focus." Once you're clear yourself on expectations/priorities, you must clearly communicate that to your colleagues. How to do that? Here are my seven "Clear is Kind" guidelines.

1. *Be simple & specific.* Simply state the goals and priorities. Make things "drop dead easy" for people to understand. Simplicity and specificity takes work! Anyone can be convoluted.

2. *Be empathic.* Get into others' heads. What do they know and not know? What details do you need to include to help them wrap their mind around the thing? Are they feeling fear or confusion? If so, how can you ease their minds and provide access to the information or further training they might need?

3. *Be truthful.* If there are, for example, numbers you aren't proud of because they point to underperformance for you or your team, practice radical acceptance of what is the case, and communicate that to others in a calm and non-shaming way.

4. *Be an example.* Spend the most time and effort, yourself, on the top priorities. Are you tending to the little pots on the front of the stove, and ignoring that big pot on the back burner that will soon boil over if you don't tend to it? Stop it! It sets a bad example.

5. *Be supportive.* No one can do it all. If you really need Sally, whose plate is full, to do more of X, guide her to eliminate or simplify Y, so she has time to focus on it. Clarity is often about elimination—bye-bye good thing; hello best thing. People experience that as deeply compassionate—because again, no one can do it all.

6. *Be forthright about positive and negative outcomes.* Say, "If X doesn't get done, it's likely that Y [negative outcome] will happen." If X does get done, it's likely that Y [positive outcome] will happen.

7. *Be a listener.* Foster an environment of open communication, where your colleagues trust they can be clear with you, too. Ask them: Where are you feeling FOSA (frustrated, overwhelmed, scattered, and/or anxious)?

Questions like this will create a safe space for your team to ask questions and process ideas—which will increase clarity and boost collaboration.

Relaying and Receiving Feedback

All leaders must provide critical, corrective, or challenging feedback to people sometimes. Relaying feedback can be stressful because, again, our brains register it as a social threat. We need to consciously work with ourselves to be calm, wise, forthright, and caring in these situations.

Momentarily I'll go over how to provide corrective feedback in a connected and constructive way. First we need to see where such feedback should fit into the overall scheme of compassionate accountability.

The 5P = 1N Rule

I'm going to start out by giving you a powerful rule to follow, and then I'll explain the research behind it.

The rule is this: *For every one negative comment or interaction with a colleague, there should be five positive comments or interactions to counteract it.*

Dr. John Gottman is well known and respected for his research on intimate relationships. His studies have found an equation that determined whether couples stayed together or not: For every one negative comment/interaction there needed to be five positive interactions to counteract the one negative.

In 2004, research was published on what Gottman's 5:1 ratio would look like in the workplace. The effectiveness of 60 leadership teams was evaluated, and measured by financial performance, customer satisfaction ratings, and 360-degree feedback ratings of team members.

What decided the relative success of the teams was the ratio of positive to negative comments that the participants made to one another. The most successful teams were averaging a ratio of 5.6:1 whereas the lowest performing teams were averaging a 1:3 ratio, meaning that they were experiencing 3 negative comments for every positive one.

It's easy to think that our work relationships are so different from our personal relationships, but when it comes to interaction, they are not.

Researchers concluded:

> "The takeaway, for both leaders and peers, is simple: If you want to be part of a high-performing team, pay attention to how much praise and positivity you're doling out. If your ratio is below 5:1, you may be damaging the effectiveness of your team."

Without compassionate connection, criticism is corrosive and trust-destroying. It's no different than trying to redirect a child when you haven't spent enough time in play, smiles, laughs, projects, snuggles, hugs, and 'I love you's.' Criticism in the absence of connection will almost always backfire.

Soliciting Critical Feedback

As a leader, you should actively solicit criticism. Show you want to be challenged. Demonstrate that you're aware you're often wrong, don't see all sides, miss key points and problems and possibilities. You want opportunities to learn and grow! This will teach you how it feels to receive criticism, and it will model for others that it's not the end of the world to admit you're not perfect.

Michael Dearing, who headed up product marketing at eBay in 2002 and is now the CEO of Harrison Metal, used a simple but effective technique for getting people to criticize him. He put a little orange box with a slit on the top in a high-traffic area so that people could drop questions or feedback into it. At his all-hands meeting, he'd reach into the box, pull out some slips of paper, and respond to the feedback in an impromptu fashion. No matter how banal the query or comment, he was 'always amazingly respectful and took on each question thoughtfully.'[112]

Whatever your version of the "little orange box," here are four questions you can ask to encourage those you lead to challenge you.

1. What do you like most about working here? What do you like least?

2. If you were in charge, what would you change immediately?

3. What could I do or stop doing to make your life better?

4. Do any of our processes seem inefficient to you? How can we fix them?

Asking questions like these lays important groundwork for those you lead to be receptive to your critical feedback in the future.

What if somebody criticizes you in a way that feels jarring and unmerited? Oh, they will, if you invite it! When that happens, your job is to listen with the intent to understand, and then find a way to express your appreciation for their brave forthrightness. Your example of gratitude in the face of criticism will build their courage to receive back from you and others in the future.

Providing Critical Feedback

Steve Jobs once said:

> *"The most important thing I think you can do for somebody who's really good and who's really being counted on is to point out to them when they're not—when their work isn't good enough. And to do it very clearly and to articulate why—and to get them back on track."*[113]

Notice Jobs' mid-sentence correction. As leaders, it is never okay to communicate to people that *they're* not good enough. Rather, we point to ways in which *their work* isn't good enough. There's an art form to this skill, and the first and most basic guideline is to avoid personalizing. Don't make it about the person's character, personality, or essence. Make it about their choices, their actions and inactions, their work, their words. Here are three more rules of thumb for providing critical feedback to colleagues.

- *Be Specific.* As in: Why does that project need more work, and in what ways? Research shows that negative messages that are specific, even though they are painful, are better received in the long term when there is a mutual understanding of commitment and making things better.[114] Vagueness erodes trust, directness builds it.

- *Don't Criticize in Public.* It goes without saying that a 1-on-1 is the place for relaying critical feedback to someone—not a team meeting. No one wants all eyes on them while they're digesting critical feedback.

- *Encourage Responsibility.* When someone says "Ahhh, yep! I own it, I see what went wrong, I take responsibility for it, I'll fix it." *That* is the very definition of accountability. That's where you're going, that's what you're looking for. Anytime you see that flavor of response coming from someone, tell them you're in their corner, and you're there for them if they need you while they work on all the fix-its.

Compassionate Leadership in the Wake of a Mistake

Let's get back to the opening story. Remember Kate? My CFO friend whose colleague made a $2M mistake?

Kate is one of the strongest and most effective leaders I know. When I asked her how she handled meeting with this employee after learning what had happened, she said she took a deep breath and just followed her five points for corrective conversations. Here they are.

1. *Catharsis first (and elsewhere).* Do all your yelling, kicking, screaming, and swearing beforehand so it doesn't come out in the meeting. Being in active "jerk mode" with folks is counterproductive. People just shut down.

2. *Say it like it is.* The very first thing you say is, "I have to have a difficult conversation with you." Compassionate leaders do not beat around the bush. Telling the truth is kind, even if the truth is hard.

3. *Listen.* Kate's question here is, "Help me understand why you chose [whatever thing they chose to do/say that led to the screw-up]." Then listen, with openness. Kate says she sometimes learns that there are factors she wasn't aware of that led up to the mistake. In this situation, there definitely were. It wasn't fully Dave's fault. There were, in fact, others who should have been overseeing the process,

but were not. The person who makes the biggest mistake is the person who deserves the deepest listening, because their story contains a roadmap for how to do better.

4. *Don't define them by their worst moment.* Kate was livid when she discovered the mistake, but she refused to look at this employee and see only "FAILURE." One of the things she often says to folks who make a mistake, or aren't performing, is this: "We hired you for a reason. What are the roadblocks I can help remove so that you can step fully into best, here?"

5. *Show them how to make it right.* Kate always ends her meeting by helping the person understand the steps they need to take to correct their mistake. What do they need to do? By what time? After making a mistake, most people find it comforting to see a clear path toward fixing the issue. That's what you can help them find. Strive to relay new, remedial expectations in a straightforward but human way.

Compassionate Accountability Mantras

The way we talk to ourselves in the privacy of our own minds matters. Self-talk can make or break good leadership. Here are four mantras my clients have found helpful. May they nourish and encourage you in your ongoing quest to do hard things with heart.

1. *"Niceness-itis leads to crisis."*[115] We sometimes think we should just be nice so everyone gets along. This just shuts down the kind of work environment where people can be honest about stuff that needs to get better. *Niceness-itis* dulls a team, slows processes, and hinders performance. Toxic niceness also makes people feel insecure—direct reports don't know where they really stand, because

they just get a bunch of general, rosy "good job" stuff that doesn't help them get better. They're deprived of opportunities to learn and grow.

2. *"I'd rather be trusted than liked."* The most pressing question you should be asking yourself isn't "Do my team members like me?" It's "Do my team members trust me?" It's natural to worry about what people think of us. We're all focused on being liked, and we fear being rejected. However, when you're overly worried about how people perceive you, you're less willing to say and do the things that will truly strengthen your team—and that reticence will erode trust over time.

3. *"It's time to give a damn."* As leaders of people, it's easy to feel too tired and overloaded to care or argue. As in: "She'll feel good if I tell her I liked her dumb flowchart, and that will make my life easier than explaining why it made no sense." Exhaustion leads us down these roads sometimes, but leaders must do better. They must find the courage and grit to give a damn. And if you find you just don't have the bandwidth to do so? Talk to your leader about it. Ask for help finding space, time, and motivation to correct those you lead when it's needed.

4. *"It's not mean, it's clear."*[116] We've all grown up hearing, "If you don't have anything nice to say, don't say anything at all." One of the reasons being a boss is hard is because it's your job to tell people when they're screwing up, doing it wrong, and not showing up like you need them to. There's a lot of unlearning we need to do because we think being challenging and direct is mean. It's not. Honest, critical feedback—when it comes from a place of genuine care and connection—is a massive gift to everyone, both individually and collectively.

Discussion Questions

1. In what ways would you like to experience greater clarity in your personal and professional life? Can you identify specific situations or circumstances when you feel unclear, and what factors contribute to that?

2. How do you plan to remind yourself of the 5P = 1N rule and apply it within your workplace? Does your work culture provide a supportive environment for critical feedback and open communication?

3. Can you think of a leader in your own life who relays difficult and/or corrective feedback with a high amount of connection and care? Share your thoughts on the significance of compassionate feedback and its potential impact on individuals and teams.

CHAPTER 16
COMPASSIONATE LEADERSHIP AMID CONFLICT AND TRAUMA

In this final chapter, I want to leave you with some actionable strategies that will empower you to navigate conflict and societal trauma. In our modern world, both are inevitable aspects of life and leadership. Let's explore how to handle them with wise, fierce compassion.

Leading Amid Conflict

We all have goals—things we want to accomplish or realize in our lives, teams, and careers. According to psychologist Kurt Lewin, the definition of conflict centers on the clash of goals.[117] When one person's (or group's) pursuit of their aims is interrupted or interfered with by another, conflict happens.

Healthy organizations and teams house a beautiful diversity of talents, perspectives, personalities, cultures, and aims. Because of this, goals *will* clash. Conflict is inescapable. As a leader, it's your job to navigate conflict with compassionate wisdom—with empathic awareness and agile, resolution-bringing decisiveness.

Easier said than done, right? For many, conflict is deeply triggering. Social tension activates the threat detection system in the human nervous system, which can swiftly send you into fight/flee/freeze/fawn mode. If conflict wasn't handled well in your family of origin growing up, you can expect more intense triggering when differences of personality or opinion arise in your professional life.

Rest assured, all conflict is workable. More than this, it's often an incredible opportunity for growth and innovation. Every conflict offers a chance to model compassionate action amid challenge, which heightens trust and teaches the people you lead that difficulties can be transcended.

With some mindful intentionality and self-compassionate awareness, we can calmly and consciously *choose* how to respond when goals are threatened or thwarted.

Following are eight principles for leaders looking to model wisdom and compassion during conflict. If you follow these guidelines, you'll lower the likelihood that conflict will bring significant or lasting harm. More than this, you'll increase the chances that the clash of goals will produce learning, growth, and transformation.

1. Don't Shy Away

Evolving things will, by default, experience some amount of tension, chaos, and disorganization. This is true of everything from individual cells to large organizations to complex ecosystems. *All* self-organizing systems live and develop by having to re-constitute themselves, over and over, in the face of crisis.[118]

So don't be afraid to lean into the tension. It's not necessarily a sign that something is wrong. As uncomfortable and unpredictable as it is, conflict really can be a place where something innovative starts to take shape.

2. Set a Positive, Empathetic Tone

Relationship researcher, John Gottman, has revealed the importance of the mood or tone at the start of a conflict. Positive emotions like gentle humor, interest, curiosity, and affection make negative communication less harmful in relationships. People feel connected and humanized. They're less likely to leave the disagreement feeling hurt.

Don't forget empathy. When you actively tune into the emotions and perspectives of the people you lead, it de-escalates negativity. Empathizing means communicating, verbally and nonverbally: "I see you, I hear you, I get you." Empathy isn't necessarily about agreement; it's about showing respect.

3. Stand in Your Integrity

According to Dr. Brené Brown, being in your integrity means "you choose courage over comfort. You choose what's right over what is fun, fast, or easy. And you choose to practice your values rather than simply professing them."[119]

In my life I've sometimes felt terrified of standing in my integrity. What if someone doesn't accept me, approve of me, or like what I have to say? I come from a long line of white midwestern women with Scandinavian ancestors—which means, in conflict, I'm good at hiding emotions, masking my opinions to match yours (to keep peace), harboring resentment, and later, being splendidly passive-aggressive.

Nevertheless, I've learned over the years that it harms me and others when I try to make the conflict go away by staging a disappearing act—when I nod and feign agreement. It's cowardly and disrespectful. Later, when the person finds me singing a different tune, they're rightfully confused and hurt. Sometimes they even feel unsafe around me. Safe, trustworthy people stand in their own truth while empathically reaching out and letting the truth of someone else touch them, challenge them, and change them—but not erase them.

Compassionate conflict requires us to know who we are and what our current truth is. It requires us to be willing to stand alone in it. This isn't easy because we must let go of trying to control what people think of us. However, this "wilderness" is, according to Dr. Brown, "the place of true belonging—the bravest and most sacred place you will ever stand."[120]

4. Set Clear Boundaries

Boundaries in conflict mean things like: Being willing to say no; being willing to state what's okay and not okay; being willing to swiftly shut down conversation if things get too ugly or hurtful so as to protect people.

One crucial boundary for compassionate conflict is a commitment to resisting dehumanization. Dehumanization happens when

159

we isolate people (or groups of people) based on certain aspects of their identity, and conclude that because of those aspects, they're not worthy of our attention, consideration, kindness, or respect. When we're seeking to be compassionate amidst conflict, resisting dehumanizing words and images, wherever they're found, is a boundary that should be in place always and without exception.

5. *Choose to Read People Generously*

In a 2019 interview with Russell Brand, Dr. Brown discusses one of her key research questions when she's studying compassion. It's this: "Do you believe, in general, that people are doing the best they can?"

Sometimes it feels easy to assume that, yes, people are doing their best. Sometimes it feels most honest to say, "Heck, no! People can do better! They can always do better!"

Here's a thought experiment. Picture someone with whom you have a problem right now. Someone whose beliefs, actions, and/or words you find difficult to tolerate. Now imagine that an all-knowing presence appeared to you and said, "This person is doing the best they can, in this moment, in their context, given their history, with the tools they have. They really are—they're doing their best." If you suddenly were fully compelled to believe this, would it shift things for you?

For me, choosing to believe someone is doing their best requires me to admit that I don't know the whole story. I don't know all the factors. When I admit this, my heart softens, my anger recedes. Instead, I open to other emotions within me— grief maybe, or fear. I find I can get curious about the factors in their life story that I may not have considered before. Suddenly I can open up to the reality of their situation, and even start to wonder if there's a way I could help rather than just judge and fume.

6. Know What to Ask and Say

When you're conversing with someone with whom you don't see eye to eye, what are some questions you can ask? What are some phrases you can use? What can you say that will ground the dialogue in respect and civility, and move it in the direction of kindness and perhaps even compassion? These are important questions for leaders because the way you relate in conflict sets an example for everyone else to follow. When circumstances are tense and tricky, people watch you with special interest as they gauge how to comport themselves. When you're just starting out, you can ask:

- *"What do you think we should intend to accomplish in this conversation?"* Agreed upon goals bring a sense of common ground, safety, and collaboration.

When you're hearing their truth, you can say things like:

- *"Tell me more."* or *"I'm curious about the experiences that led you to that point of view."* or, *"Help me understand why this matters to you so much."* These phrases communicate curiosity and respect. They don't mean you necessarily agree or condone. They do mean you're doing your best to understand.

- If appropriate, you can also say, *"Actually, I don't know a lot about that. Tell me what you know and why you care so much."* This communicates humility and prevents you from making ill-informed statements, which is never compassionate.

- You can also say, *"I think I see; thanks."* or *"I appreciate you sharing that with me."* Gratitude for the other person's frankness is a wonderful way to move the conversation forward.

When you're speaking your truth, you can say things like:

- *"At this point, my stance on that is—"* Our views shift throughout our lives; that's only human. It's humble, honest, and deeply mature to admit that.

- You can also say, *"Let me tell you a story about how I came to think/believe this."* or *"The reason I feel so strongly about X is that I very much value Y."* *"Speaking for myself—"* Show the other person that you know yourself and your context; you own your story and views; and you're speaking from your own truth—not on behalf of anyone else.

- You can also say, *"What I just said isn't quite right. Let me try again."* If you catch yourself either hiding your opinion or overstating it, then interrupt yourself and get on some clearer, more authentic ground.

- You can also say, *"Ouch!"* If something the other person said hurt you, use the immediacy of the moment to let them know. This is part of having good boundaries.

When you're pivoting, you can say things like:
- *"Can we pause there for a moment? I need a minute to ponder."* Creating space for silence during a conflicted conversation is almost always a wise move.

- You can also say, *"No, that's a line. I can't go there with you."* Once again, being clear about boundaries is essential. Taking the high road is essential. Remember, the opposite of compassion is to let someone run roughshod over you or others.

- You can also say, *"Aha, there we are on common ground."* Naming points of agreement creates a sense of concord and mutual understanding.

- You can also say, "*What grieves me most about that is—*" It's easier to be angry than grieved, but grief is more real, and sharing it opens space in conversations that anger never could.

- You can also say, "*I have to be done now.*" It's alright to walk away if things have devolved. Sometimes this is the most compassionate, high-road action you can take.

7. Understand How Your Personality Impacts Your Conflict Approach

Decades of research into the "Big Five" personality traits show that some people are naturally more agreeable than others. Some people are naturally more open to new ideas than others. Some people are naturally more positive and confident than others. Some people are naturally more outgoing and energetic than others, and some people are naturally more disciplined and organized than others.

Self-awareness regarding your personality tendencies is a power skill when it comes to leading well through conflict. If you don't know where you score on the "Big Five," find one of the many free online assessments and take ten minutes to find out. Then, for instance, if you discover you're naturally low on agreeableness, you can consciously curb your inclination to be detached and cantankerous. You can choose to work on being welcoming and understanding instead.

8. Understand How Your Attachment Style Impacts Your Conflict Approach

Developmental psychologists have long known that our early attachment experiences with caregivers impact our social relationships as adults. This is especially true in the realm of conflict. There are four main attachment styles: Dismissing, fearful, secure, and preoccupied.

Dismissing	Fearful
Avoidant, detached	Dramatic, erratic
Freeze/Flee	Fight/Flee
Secure	**Preoccupied**
Confident, calm	Anxious, clingy
Emotionally regulated	Freeze/Fawn

◊ HC

If our general attachment style is "secure," we tend to navigate conflict well. We can stay connected to the other person while we hold our ground. We are confident, calm, non-reactive, resilient, and tolerant of discomfort. In the face of social threat, we can remain emotionally regulated.

If our general attachment style is "dismissing," we're often tempted to become *avoidant and detached* in adult relationships. We absolutely hate conflict—it drains us deeply because it feels like we're going to get swallowed up in the social tension. When conflict happens, we might get stony or dismissive or utilize the silent treatment. It's a freeze/flee response to social threat.

If our general attachment style is "preoccupied," we're often tempted to become *anxious* and *clingy* in adult relationships. We're terrified of conflict—it scares us deeply because it feels like we might get rejected and abandoned. When conflict happens, we might get apologetic or clingy or indecisive or utilize emotional manipulation. It's a freeze/fawn response to social threat.

If our general attachment style is "fearful," we're often tempted to become *dramatic* and *erratic* in adult relationships. Conflict makes us feel internally disorganized—we fear being rejected ourselves, but we're more than happy to reject the other person. When conflict happens, we might get explosive, aggressive, or cruelly dismissive. It's a fight/flee response to social threat.

Knowing your attachment style is key to leading well through conflict. For example, if you know you're naturally *dismissing* and prone to using the silent treatment, you can consciously work to stay more connected, empathic, and get comfortable with being present and reassuring. Or, if you know you're naturally *preoccupied* and prone to being overly clingy and apologetic, you can consciously work to distance yourself—not apologize if it's not necessary—and get more comfortable with people not liking you.

Compassionate Leadership Amid Collective Trauma

Pandemics. Natural disasters. Political upheavals. Recent events have forced leaders to ask what their role is when the world brings heightened levels of suffering and uncertainty.

In the face of a traumatic event that affects many, it's crucial that leaders take swift action to set into motion the healing process. People will be looking to those at the helm of the organization for empathy, reassurance, and practical assistance amid the chaos.

In their extensive research on compassionate leadership, Dr. Jane E. Dutton and colleagues[121] have found that compassionate leadership amidst trauma is about creating a "context for meaning"—an environment in which people can give free and open expression to their questions and feelings surrounding a traumatic event. Deep pain brings existential angst. People wonder: Why did this happen? Could I have prevented it? How will I cope? What's the greater significance of this?

Of course, leaders can't be expected to answer these questions for people, but leaders *can* create a holding environment for them to be worked through. The message you want to send is something like this: "I understand that this event raises big questions and stirs up big emotions. This is a place where you will be supported as you search for ways to make meaning and find your best strategies for coping." Perhaps setting up a weekly luncheon or virtual roundtable—a "brave space" of safety where people can process emotions in a judgment-free and supportive zone—would be a good place to begin.

Three Key Insights for Navigating Collective Trauma

In her TED Talk on "How to Turn Climate Anxiety Into Action[122]," psychologist Dr. Renée Lertzman shares three vital insights that I believe hold valuable lessons for navigating collective trauma within the workplace.

First, *understand your Window of Tolerance*. How much stress can you tolerate before becoming dysregulated—either shutting down or responding rigidly? When we exceed our window, it inhibits our ability to be resilient and adaptive, which are crucial for taking effective action. This challenge is playing out globally, as people worldwide struggle to process the flood of distressing climate and political information.

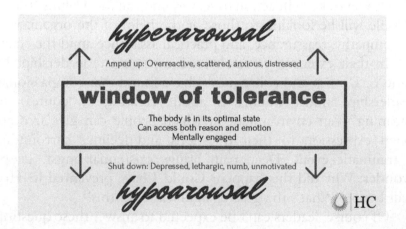

Second, *acknowledge the double bind*. Each new piece of societal data or bad news that we take in ends up pushing us outside of our window of tolerance. We care deeply, yet also feel scared, powerless, and unsure of where to start. This "damned if you do, damned if you don't" predicament is an intensely intolerable human experience. From the outside, this can appear as apathy or lack of motivation. As leaders, it's important to recognize that this outward response often masks the complex emotional landscape beneath the surface. Trying to simply provide solutions or increase motivation may backfire, as it fails to address the deeper psychological factors at play.

Third, *cultivate attunement*. The antidote to this double bind is attunement—the feeling of being deeply understood and accepted exactly as we are. When we can approach ourselves and others with this level of compassion, we become far more capable of solving problems, tapping into our creativity, and rising to meet challenges.

What if our workplaces, communities, and society at large adopted this framework? It starts with turning inward—being compassionate with ourselves, and understanding our own emotional landscapes. From that foundation of self-awareness, we can then attune to those around us, creating the conditions for authentic dialogue, collaborative problem-solving, and collective resilience.

A Context for Action in Traumatic Circumstances

In traumatic situations, leaders can also help create a "context for action"—an environment in which pain can be alleviated. Practical support matters a great deal. Here are a few examples:

- Renting a hotel room for a few nights for an employee who needs to be away from home because a loved one has been hospitalized.

- Beginning a meal train for a colleague who has been hit especially hard by the stress of the situation.

- Redirecting funds intended for other purposes to pay for on-site (or remotely accessible) grief counselors in times of collective trauma.

Finally, in traumatic times, it's crucial for leaders to be courageously vulnerable. Remember, *leaders set emotion norms* in organizations. If they themselves are expressing their humanity amid the crisis, this implicitly communicates to others that they can do the same and receive support. Witnessing a leader being vulnerable about their own story and experience can be a powerfully healing thing for those who witness it—especially during times of acute pain.

Discussion Questions

1. Conflict is an inevitable aspect of leadership, and being prepared for it is crucial. Among the eight principles outlined in this chapter, which principles resonated with you the most? How do you envision keeping these principles as essential resources for yourself when you encounter conflict in the future?

2. In the context of dealing with collective trauma, how do you perceive these eight principles being manifested? Can you envision their potential impact within the workplace? How might applying these principles contribute to healing and resilience in the face of collective trauma?

3. Upon completing this book, what is the most significant takeaway for you? What key insights, ideas, or perspectives are you walking away with? How do you anticipate incorporating or applying these takeaways in your personal and professional life moving forward?

AFTERWORD
HUMAN BEING FIRST

Around the middle of the last century there lived a Minnesota farm boy named Jerry. Jerry was always on the small and skinny side, a bit shy, and never very good in school, but he knew how to work and he was a whiz with machinery.

After high school, Jerry tried college, but dropped out after a few semesters. He got a job working on the floor at Federal Cartridge—an ammunition plant in Anoka, Minnesota. This suited him just fine. When he was twenty, Jerry's girlfriend, Tess, got pregnant, so they married. This was the 1960s, and that's what people often did then. The couple had three kids in the space of five years.

Life was going along fine until Tess became sick—very sick. As it turned out, she had a fatal liver disorder. At the tender age of twenty-four, Jerry found himself a widower with three heartbroken children under the age of five.

Jerry's boss at Federal was a guy named RB. "Old RB," as he'd come to be affectionately known, had been the one to hire Jerry years before. He'd seen something in Jerry. Here was a young man with a sharp mechanical intelligence, and a burn-in-the-belly ambition. RB liked how Jerry was easy to laugh, quick to lend a hand, willing to dream big, and not afraid to work hard. This kid had promise.

The truth is, by the time young Jerry lost his wife, Old RB was more than a boss. He'd become a mentor.

After Tess's death, RB watched Jerry struggle to hold on to himself. He'd become distant from his kids, dropping them off at his parents for long stretches. He'd become irritable and withdrawn. He started coming in later to work, clearly hungover

171

from another night closing out the bar. RB cared about this kid and really felt for what he must be going through. He gave it some time, but after a while, he had to admit he was angry. The ire wasn't just about the underperformance at work. The worst part was that Jerry seemed to have given up on himself. He'd succumbed to hopelessness and despair.

One day, RB pulled Jerry aside and he said this. "Kid, I know you're going through some things I can't even begin to imagine. And I feel for you; I really do. But you're late every day, you're nowhere near production quota, and everyone here knows you're drinking too much. Besides that, you're burdening your Ma and Pa with raising your kids at a time when they need their dad more than ever. So here's how it is. If you keep this up, you've got a pink slip coming any day. More importantly, those kids need you, and I know how important fatherhood is to you. So it's time to do something about your boozin', and start showing up for those little kids. And, by the way, I've been going to the AA group at St. Stephens for years. If you'd ever like to come, we'd love to have you."

I grew up hearing stories of Old RB because Jerry was the man who raised me— my stepdad, Gerald J. Bauer. RB gave my dad the compassionate attention, care, and accountability my dad needed to find hope again during the darkest, most traumatizing moment of his life. RB saw my dad. Empathized with my dad— and then acted with courageous care by saying hard things with heart.

Dad went on to find healing, hope, and sobriety. In time, he became Vice President of Federal Cartridge. In that role, he carried on RB's legacy of humanizing leadership. Dad transformed many lives with his forthright, big-hearted approach to supporting and developing the people in his charge. He took a special interest in individuals going through difficult life circumstances, and those whose pain occluded their awareness of their own present abilities and future potentials.

Dad passed away in 2018 from a rare neurodegenerative disease. Recently, I tracked down a former colleague of my dad's,

Kitty Keniston, who said this of him: "Jerry would say it like it is, with no bullshit, then love you to pieces. He had the biggest heart in the world. He was one of the best leaders we ever had at Federal."

Permission to Care

The stories about RB, my dad, and Kitty illustrate the power of a leadership style that puts a premium on real, intentional, compassionate connection between people. In a time when our lives and workplaces are brimming over with stress, volatility, uncertainty, and struggle, compassionate leadership is what we most need.

There's still a good deal of resistance to this, however. When I work with leaders on compassionate leadership, one of the most common responses I get is *relief.* People are so happy to learn all the reasons why they not only *can,* but *should* care about the people they lead. As one executive put it, "Your training program gave me what I've long craved—*permission to care.*"

Despite so much emphasis on emotional intelligence and belonging in organizations, many leaders still feel an unspoken pressure to keep their distance, sanitize conversations, project cool aloofness, and keep things "strictly business." When they learn about the evidence-backed benefits of leading like RB and my dad, they often feel as though someone has lifted a heavy burden from their shoulders. It makes sense. It's hard work to suppress our natural desire to form real bonds with the people around us. How freeing to know that we can just go with that desire!

Human Being First

Many of us have heard it said, "Live each day like it's your last." It's an incredibly inspiring exhortation and it puts everything into perspective very, very quickly.

Author, speaker, and leadership expert, Og Madino, suggests that we try out another saying: "Treat each person as if it's their last day on earth."

Imagine for a minute that the most difficult person on your team is going to die. Tomorrow. How will that change how you interact with them? Will you show them a bit more attention and appreciation? A bit more empathy and goodwill? A bit more genuine gratitude and even love, than you ever have before?

Now. Expand that out. What if that saying became a way of life—not just for today, but for tomorrow, and the next day, and the day after that?

We don't know what people are going through and we don't know what kind of run they've got left ahead of them. So what if we put a big HUMAN BEING FIRST lens over every other role these people on our teams occupy?

Before there's another Sales Director whose quarterly numbers are disappointingly low: HUMAN BEING FIRST. Before there's *yet another* PTO request coming through: HUMAN BEING FIRST. Before there's one more mid-year review for which to prepare; one more sick day being called in; one more communication blunder: HUMAN BEING FIRST.

It's a subtle inward shift. A change of heart and perspective. It might not immediately alter anything about your outward leadership activities or plans. However, I guarantee it will change your presence, the way people experience you.

"Compassionate people," said Albert Einstein, "are geniuses in the art of living, more necessary to the dignity, security, and joy of humanity than the discoverers of knowledge." Whatever your leadership role in your organization and beyond, may you be empowered to be more and more a genius in the precious art of life and leadership.

We are, *all* of us, *always*, human beings first.

Notes

1. Nicole Bullock and Jo Constanz, "They're in a State of Fear: Quiet Quitting is Scaring CEOs," *Seattle Times* (Sept. 23, 2022), updated Sept. 26, 2022, accessed March 13, 2023 at https://www.seattletimes.com/business/theyre-in-a-state-of-fear-quiet-quitting-is-striking-fear-in-ceos

2. Jim Harter, "Is Quiet Quitting Real?" Gallup Workplace, September 6, 2022, Updated May 17, 2023. Accessed November 6, 2023 at https://www.gallup.com/workplace/398306/quiet-quitting-real.aspx#:~:text=%22Quiet%20quitters%22%20make%20up%20at,description%20%2D%2D%20could%20get%20worse

3. Jason Furman and Wilson Powell III, "Record US Productivity Slump in First Half of 2022 Risks Higher Inflation and Unemployment," Peterson Institute for International Economics, August 9, 2022. Accessed March 1, 2023 at https://www.piie.com/blogs/realtime-economics/record-us-productivity-slump-first-half-2022-risks-higher-inflation-and?utm_source=npr_newsletter&utm_medium=email&utm_content=20220909&utm_term=7224424&utm_campaign=money&utm_id=5861281&orgid=88&utm_att1=

4. Reade Pickert, "US Productivity Declines more Than Forecast, Labor Costs Climb." Bloomberg, May 4, 2023. Accessed November 6, 2023 at https://www.bloomberg.com/news/articles/2023-05-04/us-productivity-declines-more-than-forecast-labor-costs-climb#xj4y7vzkg

5. "Media Tip Sheet: Managers Should Embrace 'Quiet Quitting,'" GW Media Relations, August 26, 2022. Accessed March 1, 2023 at https://mediarelations.gwu.edu/media-tip-sheet-managers-should-embrace-quiet-quitting

6. Adam Grant, "There's a Name for the Blah You're Feeling: It's Called Languishing," *New York Times* (April 19, 2021), accessed March 16, 2023 at: https://www.nytimes.com/2021/04/19/well/mind/covid-mental-health-languishing.html

7. A term first coined by the U.S. Army War College in the aftermath of the Cold War, VUCA stands for volatility, uncertainty, complexity, and ambiguity.

8. Rasmus Hougaard and Jacqueline Carter, *Compassionate Leadership: How to Do Hard Things in a Human Way*. Boston, MA: Harvard Business Review Press, 2022.

9. Jane E., Dutton, Peter J. Frost, Monica C. Worline, Jacoba M. Lilius, and Jason M. Kanov, "Leading in times of Trauma," *Harvard Business Review* 80, no. 1 (2002): 54-61.

10. https://www.stress.org/workplace-stress

11. https://www.qualtrics.com/blog/confronting-mental-health

12. Gallup Workplace, "State of the Global Workplace: 2023 Report." Accessed November 6, 2023 at https://www.gallup.com/workplace/349484/state-of-the-global-workplace.aspx

13. Ibid

14. "Highlights: Workplace Stress & Anxiety Disorders Survey," Anxiety & Depression Association of America, accessed March 23, 2023 at https://adaa.org/workplace-stress-anxiety-disorders-survey

15. "49% of U.S. Workers Are Struggling with Alcohol and Substance Abuse," Business Wire (April 1, 2021), accessed March 23, 2023 @ https://www.businesswire.com/news/home/20210401005098/en/49-of-U.S.-Workers-Are-Struggling-with-Alcohol-and-Substance-Abuse

16. American Addiction Centers Editorial Staff, "The Prevalence of Substance Abuse in the Workplace," March 3, 2023, updated March 25, 2023, accessed March 23, 2023 at https://drugabuse.com/addiction/substance-abuse-workplace

17. Kelli Mason, "Survey: More than 1 in 4 Have Quit a Job Because of Their Mental Health," JobSage (April 1, 2022), accessed March 23, 2023 at https://www.jobsage.com/blog/survey-do-companies-support-mental-health

18. Paul Gilbert, "Compassion: Universally Misunderstood" HuffingtonPost (August 25, 2016), accessed September 27, 2023 at: https://www.huffingtonpost.co.uk/professor-paul-gilbert-obe/compassion-universally-misunderstood_b_8028276.html?guccounter=1].

19. Rasmus Hougaard and Jacqueline Carter, *Compassionate Leadership: How to Do Hard Things in a Human Way* (Boston: Harvard Business Review Press, 2022), 1.

20. Hougaard and Carter, *Compassionate Leadership*, 20.

21. James N. Baron and Michael T. Hannan, Organizational Blueprints for Success in High-Tech Start-Ups: Lessons from the Stanford Project on Emerging Companies," *California Management Review* 44, no. 3 (2002): 8-36.

22. Weng, Helen Y., Andrew S. Fox, Alexander J. Shackman, Diane E. Stodola, Jessica Z. K. Caldwell, Matthew C. Olson, Gregory M. Rogers, and Richard J. Davidson. "Compassion Training Alters Altruism and Neural Responses to Suffering." *Psychological Science* 24, no. 7 (July 2013): 1171–80.

23. Mongrain, Myriam, Jacqueline Chin, and Leah Shapira. "Practicing Compassion Increases Happiness and Self-Esteem." *Journal of Happiness Studies* 12, no. 6 (December 2011): 963–81. https://doi.org/10.1007/s10902-010-9239-1.

24. Adam Waytz, Hal E. Hershfield, and Diana I. Tamir, "Mental Simulation and Meaning in Life," *Journal of Personality and Social Psychology* 108, no. 2 (2018): 336-355.

25. Fredrickson, B.L., M.A. Cohn, K.A. Coffey, J. Pek, and S.M. Finkel. 2008. Open hearts build lives: Positive emotions, induced through loving-kindness meditation, build consequential personal resources. *Journal of Personality and Social Psychology* 95 (5): 1045–1062. https://doi.org/10.1037/a0013262.

26. Klimecki, O., T. Singer, B. Oakley, A. Knafo, G. Madhavan, and D. S. Wilson. "Empathic distress fatigue rather than compassion fatigue? Integrating findings from empathy research in psychology and social neuroscience," *Pathological Altruism*, Oxford University Press, (2012): 368-383.

27. Olga M. Klimecki, Susanne Leiberg, Claus Lamm, Tania Singer, Functional Neural Plasticity and Associated Changes in Positive Affect After Compassion Training, *Cerebral Cortex*, Volume 23, Issue 7, July 2013, Pages 1552–1561, https://doi.org/10.1093/cercor/bhs142

28. Galante, J., Galante, I., Bekkers, M.-J., & Gallacher, J. (2014). Effect of kindness-based meditation on health and wellbeing: A systematic review and meta-analysis. *Journal of Consulting and Clinical Psychology*, 82(6), 1101–1114. https://doi.org/10.1037/a0037249

29. Tingey, J. L., McGuire, A. P., Stebbins, O. L., & Erickson, T. M. (2019). Moral elevation and compassionate goals predict posttraumatic growth in the context of a college shooting. The *Journal of Positive Psychology*, 14(3), 261–270. https://doi.org/10.1080/17439760.2017.1402077.

30. Konrath, S., Fuhrel-Forbis, A., Lou, A., & Brown, S. (2012). Motives for volunteering are associated with mortality risk in older adults. *Health Psychology*, 31(1), 87–96. https://doi.org/10.1037/a0025226

31. Bellosta, Batalla, Miguel, Ausiàs Cebolla, Blasco, Josefa Pérez, and Albiol, Luis Moya. 2021. "Introducing Mindfulness and Compassion-based Interventions to Improve Verbal Creativity in Students of Clinical and Health Psychology." *Psychology & Psychotherapy: Theory, Research & Practice* 94 (3): 541–57. doi:10.1111/papt.12329.

32. Dundas, Ingrid, Per-Einar Binder, Tia G.B. Hansen, and Signe Hjelen Stige. "Does a Short Self-Compassion Intervention for Students Increase Healthy Self-Regulation?" *Scandinavian Journal of Psychology* 58, no 5 (2017): 443-450.

33. Sirois, F. M., Molnar, D. S., & Hirsch, J. K. (2015). Self-compassion, stress, and coping in the context of chronic illness. *Self and Identity*, 14(3), 334–347. https://doi.org/10.1080/15298868.2014.996249

34. Joanna J. Arch, Kirk Warren Brown, Derek J. Dean, Lauren N. Landy, Kimberly D. Brown, and Mark L. Laudenslager, "Self-Compassion Training Modulates Alpha-Amylase, Heart Rate Variability, and Subjective Responses to Social Evaluative Threat in Women," *Psychoneuroendocrinology* 42 (2014): 49-58.

35. Baron and Hannan, 30.

36. The information in this section is derived from publicly available news sources and press releases, as well as a one-hour webinar put on by *Potential Project* and *Harvard Business Review*. The webinar, held on March 10, 2023, was titled "Leadership Re-Imagined: Uncertainty, Compassion, and Why We Need More Women Leaders." It was composed of a three-way conversation between Maynard, Jacqueline Carter, and Julie Devoll.

37. https://theorg.com/iterate/what-is-the-real-cost-of-the-great-resignation#the-real-cost-of-the-great-resignation

38. Julia Herbst, "If You Hate Your Job, You're Not Alone. Everyone is Experiencing the 'Great Gloom,'" *Fast Company* (Nov. 5, 2023). Accessed Nov. 9, 2023 at https://www.fastcompany.com/90975778/if-you-hate-job-not-alone-everyone-experiencing-great-gloom

39. Charaba, Chase. "Employee Rentention: The Real Cost of Losing and Employee." *PeopleKeep*. February 2, 2023. Accessed February 23, 2023. https://www.peoplekeep.com/blog/employee-retention-the-real-cost-of-losing-an-employee.

40. Wagner, Rodd and Jim Harter. "The Fifth Great Element of Managing." *Gallup Business Journal*. September 13, 2007. Accessed February 23, 2023. https://news.gallup.com/businessjournal/28561/fifth-element-great-managing.aspx

41. Cengage Research Group. "What's Driving the Great Resignation?" January 20, 2022. Accessed February 23, 2023. https://www.cengagegroup.com/news/press-releases/2022/great-resigners-research-report/

42. McWilliams, Lizzie. "New EY Consulting Survey Confirms 90% of US Workers Believe Empathetic Leadership Leads to Higher Job Satisfaction and 79% Agree it Decreases Employee Turnover." *Ernst & Young Global Limited*. October 14, 2021. Accessed February 23, 2023. https://www.ey.com/en_us/news/2021/09/ey-empathy-in-business-survey

43. Shanahan, Jon. "2022 State of Workplace Empathy Executive Summary." Businesssolver. January, 2023. Accessed February 23, 2022. https://www.businessolver.com/workplace-empathy/

44. McWilliams, Lizzie. "New EY Consulting Survey Confirms 90% of US Workers Believe Empathetic Leadership Leads to Higher Job Satisfaction and 79% Agree it Decreases Employee Turnover." *Ernst & Young Global Limited*. October 14, 2021. Accessed February 23, 2023.

45. Van Bommel, Tara. "The Power of Empathy in Times of Crisis and Beyond." *Catalyst*. 2020. Accessed February 23, 2023. https://www.catalyst.org/reports/empathy-work-strategy-crisis

46. Hougard and Carter, *Compassionate Leadership*

47. Ibid.

48. As reported in the July 27, 2022 episode of *Empowering Workplaces* with Maddie Grant and Sanja Licina: https://open.spotify.com/

49. DNA of engagement. (n.d.). The Conference Board. https://www. conference-board.org/topics/dna-of-engagement

50. Barsade, S. G., & O'Neill, O. A. (2014). What's Love Got to Do with It? A Longitudinal Study of the Culture of Companionate Love and Employee and Client Outcomes in a Long-term Care Setting. Administrative Science Quarterly, 59(4), 551- 598. https:// doi.org/10.1177/0001839214538636

51. Boyatzis, R. E., Passarelli, A., Koenig, K. A., Lowe, M. J., Mathew, B., Stoller, J. K., & Phillips, M. D. (2012). Examination of the neural substrates activated in memories of experiences with resonant and dissonant leaders. *Leadership Quarterly*, 23(2), 259–272. https://doi.org/10.1016/j.leaqua.2011.08.003

52. Catalyst. (2023, October 19). The Power of Empathy in Times of Crisis and Beyond (Report) | Catalyst. https://www.catalyst.org/ reports/empathy-work- strategy-crisis

53. McWilliams, L. (2021, October 14). New EY Consulting survey confirms 90% of US workers believe empathetic leadership leads to higher job satisfaction. EY: Building a Better World. https://www. ey.com/en_us/news/2021/09/ey-empathy-in-business-survey

54. Ibid.

55. Q5 of Gallup's Q12 employee engagement survey asks about employee's experiences of managerial care (or lack thereof) at work. Caring, compassionate managerial connections are is a crucial element of employee engagement. Engaged workers have 41% lower absenteeism rates, according to Gallup. Harter, B. J. (2022, August 13). Employee Engagement vs. Employee Satisfaction and Organizational Culture. Gallup.com. https://www.gallup.com/ workplace/236366/right-culture-not-employee-satisfaction.aspx

56. Australian Compassion Council, "Compassion in Leadership – The Business Case for Compassion," video podcast conversation on February 22, 2022, accessed April 7, 2023 at https://www.youtube.com/watch?v=u8DFo3lyDPA

57. Karol M. Wasylyshyn and F. Masterpasqua. "Developing Self-Compassion in Leadership Development Coaching: A Practice Model and Case Study Analysis." *International Coaching Psychology Review* 13, no. 1 (2018): 21–34.

58. Ibid., 26

59. Ibid., 28

60. Joanna J. Arch, Kirk Warren Brown, Derek J. Dean, Lauren N. Landy, Kimberly D. Brown, and Mark L. Laudenslager, "Self-Compassion Training Modulates Alpha-Amylase, Heart Rate Variability, and Subjective Responses to Social Evaluative Threat in Women," *Psychoneuroendocrinology* 42 (2014): 49-58.

61. Mayo Clinic. (2021, July 8). *Chronic stress puts your health at risk.* Mayo Clinic. https://www.mayoclinic.org/healthy-lifestyle/stress-management/in-depth/stress/art-20046037#:~:text=The%20long%2Dterm%20activation%20of

62. Neff and Germer, *The Mindful Self-Compassion Workbook*, 12.

63. Kristin Neff, *Self-Compassion: The Proven Power of Being Kind to Yourself* (New York: HarperCollins, 2011), 70.

64. For more information, visit Internal Family Systems Institute at https://ifs-institute.com/

65. Butz, Sebastian and Dagmar Stahlberg. "The Relationship Between Self-Compassion and Sleep Quality: An Overview of a Seven-Year German Research Program." *Behavioral Sciences* 10, no. 3 (2017)), 64-76.

66. Giulia Fuochi, Chiara A. Veneziani and Alberto Voci, "Exploring the Social Side of Self-Compassion: Relations With Empathy and Outgroup Attitudes," *European Journal of Social Psychology* 48, no. 6 (2018): 769-783.

67. Arch, 2014

68. Quoted in Neff, *Self-Compassion*, 118.

69. Here's an excellent online article on downregulation: https://www. goodtherapy.org/blog/biology-of-calm-how-downregulation-promotes-well-being-1027164

70. Neff and Germer, 34-36.

71. Louis Komjathy, "A Daoist Way of Being: Clarity and Stillness as Embodied Practice," *Asian Philosophy* 29, no. 1 (2019): 50-64.

72. Thich Nhat Hanh, *You Are Here: Discovering the Magic of the Present Moment* (Boulder, CO: Shambhala, 2012), 74.

73. Rick Hanson, *Buddha's Brain: The Practical Neuroscience of Happiness, Love, and Wisdom* (Oakland, CA: New Harbinger Publications, 2009), 46.

74. Pema Chödrön, *When Things Fall Apart: Heart Advice for Difficult Times* (Boston, MA: Shambhala Publications, 2000), 10-11.

75. Andrea Hollingsworth, "Implications of Interpersonal Neurobiology for a Spirituality of Compassion," *Zygon: Journal of Religion and Science* 43, no 4 (2008): 837-860.

76. Chris L. Johnson, *The Leadership Pause* (Nashville: BrainTrust Ink, 2022), 146.

77. James A. Roberts and Meredith E. David, "Boss Phubbing, Trust, Job Satisfaction and Employee Performance," Personality and Individual Differences 155, no 1 (March 2020): 109702.

78. Raja Mehtab Yasin, Sajid Bashir, Abeele, Mariek Vanden Abeele, & Jos Bartels, "Supervisor Phubbing Phenomenon in Organizations: Determinants and Impacts," *International Journal of Business Communication*, 60, no. 1 (2023): 150–172.

79. Pauline Boss, *Ambiguous Loss: Learning to Live with Unresolved Grief* (Harvard University Press, 2000).

80. Jacob B. Hirsh, Raymond A. Mar, and Jordan B. Peterson, "Psychological Entropy: A Framework for Understanding Uncertainty-Related Anxiety," *Psychological Review* 119, no. 2 (April 2012): 304–20.

81. Jin Fan, Nicholas T. Van Dam, Xiaosi Gu, Xun Liu, Hongbin Wang, Cheuk Y. Tang, and Patrick R. Hof, "Quantitative Characterization of Functional Anatomical Contributions to Cognitive Control under Uncertainty," *Journal of Cognitive Neuroscience* 26, no. 7 (July 2014): 1490–1506.

82. Nicholas R. Carleton, "The Intolerance of Uncertainty Construct in the Context of Anxiety Disorders: Theoretical and Practical Perspectives," *Expert Review of Neurotherapeutics* 12, no. 8 (August 2012): 937+; Hirsh, et al. 2012.

83. Adapted from Chris L. Johnson, *The Leadership Pause*, 153-4.

84. Chris L. Johnson, *The Leadership Pause*, 157.

85. *The Notebooks of Simone Weil*. 2 vols. Arthur Wills, trans. London: Routledge & Kegan Paul. 1956] (Dietz 1988, 133).

86. Captain D. Michael Abrashoff, *It's Your Ship: Management Techniques From the Best Damn Ship in the Navy*, Revised and Updated Edition (New York: Grand Central Publishing, 2002, 2012), 63-64.

87. Ibid.

88. A term first coined by the U.S. Army War College in the aftermath of the Cold War, VUCA stands for volatility, uncertainty, complexity, and ambiguity.

89. Louis Cozolino, *The Neuroscience of Human Relationships: Attachment and the Developing Social Brain* (New York: W.W. Norton and Company, 2006), 166.

90. Ibid.

91. Valtorta, Nicole K, Mona Kanaan, Simon Bilbody, Sara Tonzi, and Barbara Hanratty, "Loneliness and Social Isolation as Risk Factors for Coronary Heart Disease and Stoke: Systematic Review and Meta-Analysis of Longitudinal Observation Studies," *Heart* 102, no. 13 (2016): 1009-1016.

92. Rodd Wagner and Jim Harter, "The Fifth Element of Great Managing," *Gallup Business Journal*, Sept. 13, 2007, https://news.gallup.com/businessjournal/28561/fifth-element-great-managing.aspx, accessed November 23, 2023.

93. https://www.ey.com/en_us/news/2023/03/new-ey-us-consulting-study

94. Wan Abdul Rahman and Patricia Ann Castelli, "The Impact of Empathy on Leadership Effectiveness Among Business Leaders in the United States and Malaysia," *International Journal of Economics Business and Management Studies* 2, no. 3 (2013): 83-97.

95. Businesssolver, "2023 State of Workplace Empathy," Eighth Annual Report (2023), https://www.businessolver.com/workplace-empathy, accessed November 23, 2023.

96. Constantinos Coutifaris and Adam Grant, "Taking Your Team Behind the Curtain: The Effects of Leader Feedback-Sharing and Feedback-Seeking on Team Psychological Safety," *Organization Science* 33, no. 4 (2021): 1251-1699.

97. Dr. Licina mentions this research in her opening comments on the podcast *Empowering Workplaces*, "The Need for Compassionate Leadership in the Workplace," July 27, 2022.

98. Businesssolver, "2023 State of Workplace Empathy," Eighth Annual Report (2023), https://www.businesssolver.com/workplace-empathy, accessed November 23, 2023.

99. Daniel Coyle, *The Culture Code: The Secrets of Highly Successful Groups* (New York: Bantam, 2018).

100. Cozolino, *The Neuroscience of Human Relationships*, 314.

101. Jean Decety, Chia-Yan Yang, and Yawei Cheng, "Physicians Down-Regulate Their Pain Empathy Response: An Event-Related Brain Potential Study," *NeuroImage* 50, no. 4 (2010): 1676-1682; Omar Sultan Haque and Adam Waytz, "Why Doctor's Should be More Empathic – But Not Too Much More," *Scientific American* (April 26, 2011).

102. Brené Brown, *Braving the Wilderness: The Quest for True Belonging and the Courage to Stand Alone* (New York: Random House, 2017), 70-71.

103. Many (not all) of these are discussed in Nedra Glover Tawwab's wonderful book, *Set Boundaries, Find Peace: A Guide to Reclaiming Yourself* (New York: TarcherPerigee, 2021), 7.

104. NIMH. (2023, March). *Mental Illness.* National Institute of Mental Health. https://www.nimh.nih.gov/health/statistics/mental-illness.

105. Szczepanek, A. (2023, April 17). *Mind Matters: Exploring Mental Health at Work [2023 Study].* ResumeLab. https://resumelab.com/career-advice/mental-health-at-work

106. Frost, Peter J., Jane E. Dutton, Monica C. Worline, and Annette Wilson, "Narratives of Compassion in Organizations," in *Emotion in Organizations*, 2nd ed., edited by Stephen Fineman. Thousand Oakes, CA: Sage Publications (2000), 25-45.

107. Their inspiration comes from the Chinese word for busyness, which is made of two characters—one represents "killing," the other "heart."

108. Kim Scott, *Radical Candor: Be a Kick-Ass Boss Without Losing Your Humanity* (New York: St. Martin's Press, 2019), 12).

109. O. Torrès, "The Silent and Shameful Suffering of Bosses: Layoffs in SME," *International Journal of Entrepreneurship and Small Business* 13 (2011): 181-192.

110. Kim Scott, *Radical Candor: Be a Kick-Ass Boss Without Losing Your Humanity* (New York: St. Martin's Press, 2019).

111. Jim Harter, "Is Quiet Quitting Real?" *Gallup Workplace*, September 6, 2022.

112. Kim Scott, *Radical Candor*, 135

113. Quoted in Scott, 37.

114. According to Nickola Overall's research.

115. I first heard Nicola Greenway, Chief of Staff at Takeda, use the delightfully descriptive term "niceness-itis."

116. Kim Scott's phrase.

117. Derived from the theoretical framework of social psychologist Kurt Lewin.

118. As Evan Thompson describes in his brilliant book *Mind in Life* (2007).

119. Brené Brown, B*raving the Wilderness: The Quest for True Belonging and the Courage to Stand Alone* (New York: Random House, 2017).

120. Brown, *Braving the Wilderness*, 36.

121. Dutton, Jane E., Peter J. Frost, Monica C. Worline, Jacoba M. Lilius, and Jason M. Kanov. "Leading in times of Trauma." *Harvard Business Review* 80, no. 1 (2002): 54-61.

122. Accessed June 16, 2024. https://www.ted.com/talks/renee_lertz-man_how_to_turn_climate_anxiety_into_action?language=en

ABOUT THE AUTHOR

Andrea Hollingsworth is Founder and CEO of Hollingsworth Consulting and one of today's leading global experts on compassionate leadership. Since 2008, she has been studying, speaking, and writing about the science and spirituality of human emotions and relationships. Her articles have been published more than a dozen times in peer-reviewed journals, and she has taught at prestigious institutions like Princeton, Boston University, and Loyola University Chicago. In addition, Andrea has delivered talks to audiences at some of the top-ranked universities in the world—including Cambridge University in England and Heidelberg University in Germany.

Andrea spends most of her time inspiring leaders and teams to use **The Compassion Advantage**™ to build supercharged organizations through cultures of care—especially in times of challenge and change. Andrea lives with her family in Minnesota where she cheers hard at her son's soccer games and relishes every opportunity to visit the north shore of Lake Superior.

Made in the USA
Las Vegas, NV
12 November 2024

11629902R00115